Praise for

WHAT THE
CONSTITUTION
MEANS TO ME

★★★★★ "A triumph. Shattering, galvanizing, and very funny, it's one of the year's best shows."

—ALEXIS SOLOSKI, *GUARDIAN*

"Uproariously funny, wrenchingly moving, critically challenging, and politically inspiring."

—DAVID COLE, *NEW YORK REVIEW OF BOOKS*

"Risky, exposed, and excruciatingly personal. There's something delicately balanced and expansively humane about what Schreck is doing."

—SARA HOLDREN, *NEW YORK*

"In this dire moment of cultural fragmentation, Schreck is offering an oasis of connection, a place where humanity and learning are being celebrated and protected . . . Perhaps, most incredibly of all, the show offers evidence that there are still reasons to have faith in the future of America. It's a gift as improbable as it is welcome. For ninety blessed minutes, the world seems sane again."

—HOWARD FISHMAN, *NEW YORKER*

"Joy comes from watching an imaginative new kind of theater emerge . . . The best and most important play of the season."

—JESSE GREEN, *NEW YORK TIMES*

"Highlights both the brilliance and the betrayal of our Constitution (especially when it comes to women) . . . While most theater can tap into at least one feeling, Schreck rollercoasters you through every emotion before spitting you out of the theater, filled with hope."

—ASHLEY VAN BUREN, *THEATERMANIA*

"Deeply funny, heart wrenching, inspirational, and one of the most searing and enlightening pieces of political theater in recent memory."

—NAVEEN KUMAR, *TOWLEROAD*

"Grade A! Spectacular . . . The magic trick of *Constitution* is its ability to plumb the depths of despair without ever falling subject to them. It's a rollercoaster ride through genuine humor, deep sorrow, and pulsing, vibrating rage . . . *What the Constitution Means to Me* is an essential examination of our country and an urgent reminder that we should never stop holding the Constitution's (and those who've sworn to uphold it) metaphorical feet to the fire."

—MAUREEN LEE LENKER, *ENTERTAINMENT WEEKLY*

"Few new works are as instantly, trenchantly timely as this. Unique, funny, stimulating, and exquisitely heartfelt."

—DAVID ROONEY, *HOLLYWOOD REPORTER*

"It should play in every city in America."

—MICHAEL SCHULMAN, *NEW YORKER*

"Incredibly and almost excruciatingly apropos. *What the Constitution Means to Me* is moving, angry, heartbreaking, and inspiring."

—ALISSA WILKINSON, *VOX*

★★★★★ "It's more than an unmitigated success. It's a sensation."

—CASEY MINK, *BACKSTAGE*

"Hilarious and often deeply moving. *What the Constitution Means to Me* has a sense of urgency and emotional resonance."

—AMANDA MARCOTTE, *SALON*

"*What the Constitution Means to Me* is strikingly and unnervingly relevant."

—HANNAH MURPHY, *ROLLING STONE*

"An astounding success story. The best and most important play on Broadway."

—LEE SEYMOUR, *FORBES*

"Heidi Schreck's groundbreaking play *What the Constitution Means to Me* is a game changer."

—ERIN COURTNEY, *BROOKLYN RAIL*

"Endearingly funny and deeply affecting. It would be hard to identify a work for the theater with its finger more on the pulse of America right now . . . It is an act of patriotism to see it."

—PETER MARKS, *WASHINGTON POST*

★★★★★ "Inventive, invigorating, energizing, and hopeful— and exactly what our country needs."

—MELISSA ROSE BERNARDO, *NEW YORK STAGE REVIEW*

"Buoyant and stirring—the theatrical curriculum Americans desperately need now."

—CHARLES McNULTY, *LOS ANGELES TIMES*

WHAT THE CONSTITUTION MEANS TO ME

WHAT THE CONSTITUTION MEANS TO ME

HEIDI SCHRECK

THEATRE COMMUNICATIONS GROUP   NEW YORK   2020

What the Constitution Means to Me is published by Theatre Communications Group, Inc., 520 Eighth Avenue, 24th Floor, New York, NY 10018-4156

The publication of *What the Constitution Means to Me* by Heidi Schreck, through TCG's Book Program, is made possible in part by the New York State Council on the Arts with the support of Governor Andrew Cuomo and the New York State Legislature.

Special thanks to Heather Randall and the Tony Randall Theatrical Fund for their generous support of this publication.

TCG books are exclusively distributed to the book trade by Consortium Book Sales and Distribution.

Library of Congress Control Numbers:
2019020712 (print) / 2019021602 (ebook)
ISBN 978-1-55936-964-0 (paperback) / ISBN 978-1-55936-921-3 (ebook)
A catalog record for this book is available from the Library of Congress.

Cover, book design and composition by Lisa Govan
Cover photo: Jill Greenberg / Artwork: Serino Coyne

First Edition, December 2020
Second Printing, May 2023

For my mother, Sherry Chastain Schreck

ACKNOWLEDGMENTS

Special thanks to Oliver Butler for his vision and his passion; to Maria Striar and Tom Cole for seeing what was possible; and to all the talented, generous people who helped give life to this play:

Rachel Hauck, Michael Krass, Siena Zoë Allen, Jen Schriever, Sinan Refik Zafar, Raphael Mishler, Tatiana Pandiani, Sarah Lunnie, Molly Paige, Sanaz Toossi, Rosdely Ciprian, Danny Wolohan, Wisdom Kunitz, Anaya Matthews, Mike Iveson, Thursday Williams, Ben Beckley, Maria Dizzia, Jocelyn Shek, Gabriel Marin, Jessica Savage, Emilyn Toffler, Ashley-Rose Galligan, Noah Silva, Terri Kohler, Arabella Powell, Nicole Olson, Colt Luedtke, Dawn-Elin Fraser, Erin Szczechowski, and Kate Solomon-Tilley.

Everyone at Clubbed Thumb, and True Love Productions. Tony Taccone and everyone at Berkeley Rep. Jim Nicola,

Linda Chapman, Jeremy Blocker, Taylor Williams, and all the wonderful people backstage and front of house at NYTW.

Diana DiMenna, Aaron Glick, Matt Ross, Level Forward, Eva Price, Margaret Skoglund, Bethany Weinstein Stewert, Nina Essman, 321 Theatrical Management, Maximum Entertainment Productions, Carl Flanigan, and Michael Camp.

Jeni Ahlfeld, Hannah Cohen, David Dillon, McBrien Dunbar, Anthony Fladger, Aja Kane, Gregory Lynn, Katherine McCauley, Richard Ponce, Mia Roy, Darren Shaw, Gabbie Vincent, and all the wonderful people backstage and front of house at The Helen Hayes Theater.

Nicole Capatasto, Liz Lombardi, Sarah Sgro, and Claire Wojciechowski.

Maria Goyanes and Woolly Mammoth Theatre Company; Norman Lear; Sherry Chastain Schreck and Larry Schreck; Kip Fagan; Lillian and Frances Fagan-Schreck; Carl, Tanja, Sonja, and Alex Schreck; Carlo Steinman; Gloria Steinem; William Araiza; Rosa Angustia; Didi O'Connell; Scott Morfee; Morgan Gould; Sue Jean Kim; Lee Sunday Evans; Justice Ruth Bader Ginsburg; Justice Sonia Sotomayor; Sarah Gubbins; Esti Giordani; ERA Coalition; ACLU; oyez.org; everyone at Serino Coyne; Nashua New Hampshire American Legion Post 3; American Legion Post 1; American Legion Memorial Post 71; American Legion Department of Illinois; and Legal Outreach.

WHAT THE
THE CONSTITUTION
MEANS TO ME

What the Constitution Means to Me was commissioned by True Love Productions. This production originated at the Wild Project in New York City as part of Summerworks, produced by Clubbed Thumb (Maria Striar, Producing Artistic Director/Founder), in partnership with True Love Productions (Jeanne Donovan Fisher and Laurie Gilmore, Founders; Tom Cole; Darcy Stephens). It opened on June 21, 2017. It was directed by Oliver Butler. The scenic design was by Rachel Hauck, the costume design was by Michael Krass, the lighting design was by Jen Schriever, and the sound design was by Sinan Refik Zafar. The production stage manager was Ashley-Rose Galligan and the assistant stage manager was Noah Silva. The cast was:

Heidi Schreck
Rosdely Ciprian
Danny Wolohan

The West Coast premiere was produced on January 31, 2018, at Berkeley Repertory Theatre (Tony Taccone, Artistic Director; Susan Medak, Managing Director). The creative team remained the same, except the stage manager was Betsy Norton. The cast was:

Heidi Schreck
Wisdom Kunitz
Anaya Matthews
Danny Wolohan

What the Constitution Means to Me received its Off-Broadway premiere at New York Theatre Workshop (Jim Nicola, Artistic Director; Jeremy Blocker, Managing Director) on October 1, 2018. The creative team remained the same with the following changes: the associate director was Tatiana Pandiani, the assistant to the playwright and researchers were Molly Paige and Sanaz Toossi, the dramaturg was Sarah Lunnie, and the stage manager was Terri K. Kohler. The cast was:

Heidi Schreck
Rosdely Ciprian
Thursday Williams
Mike Iveson
Ben Beckley

This production transferred to Broadway at The Helen Hayes Theater on March 31, 2019 (Diana DiMenna, Aaron Glick, Matt Ross, Madeleine Foster Bersin, Myla Lerner/ Jon Bierman, Jenna Segal/Catherine Markowitz, Jana Shea/ Maley-Stollbun-Sussman, Rebecca Gold/Jose Antonio Vargas, Level Forward, Cornice Productions, Cody Lassen & Associates, and Kate Lear, producers). The creative team remained the same with the following changes: the stage manager was Arabella Powell and the assistant stage manager was Terri K. Kohler.

The Broadway production opened at The Kennedy Center for the Performing Arts Eisenhower Theater in Washington, DC, on September 13, 2019. The creative team remained the same with the following changes: the stage manager was Terri K. Kohler and the assistant stage manager was Noah Silva. The cast performed without Thursday Williams.

What the Constitution Means to Me opened on January 17, 2020, at Mark Taper Forum, Center Theatre Group (Michael Ritchie, Artistic Director; Meghan Pressman, Managing Director; Douglas C. Baker, Producing Director; Gordon Davidson, Founding Artistic Director) in Los Angeles, CA. The creative team was the same as the Kennedy Center. Eva Price was added as producer. The cast was:

Maria Dizzia
Rosdely Ciprian
Mike Iveson
Jocelyn Shek
Gabriel Marin
Jessica Savage

NOTE

After years of research, I developed large sections of this piece through extemporaneous storytelling and the style of the written text reflects this. This script is a blueprint for a living encounter, and it is essential that the performer establish a genuine and spontaneous connection with the audience. Occasional ad-libs that elide the distance between performer and audience are encouraged. This might take the form of saying "bless you" if someone sneezes or responding to audience members if they have a vocal reaction. It's also helpful for the performer to allow whatever might be happening in the country that day to affect their performance once they transition from teenager to adult.

PART ONE: THE CONTEST

Heidi enters and introduces herself to the audience. She wears a yellow blazer. The house lights are still up. She stands outside the frame of what appears to be an American Legion hall in a small, rural town. The hall is not depicted in an entirely realistic fashion; it's more like a diorama of a Legion hall that a teenage girl might have made in high school. An American flag and too many photos of Legionnaires line the walls. A live plant lurks in a corner, a reminder that although this place is filled with ghosts, it also welcomes the living.

HEIDI

Hi, I'm Heidi. Thank you all for coming out tonight.

When I was fifteen years old, I traveled the country giving speeches about the Constitution at American Legion halls for prize money. This was a scheme invented by my mom, a debate coach, to help me pay for college. I would travel to big cities like Denver and . . . Fresno, win a whole bunch of money, and then take it home to keep in my little safety deposit box for later. I was able to pay for my entire college education this way. Thank you—it was thirty years ago and it was a state school but thank you.

A few years ago, I was thinking about the Constitution and I started to wonder what exactly it was that my fifteen-year-old self loved so much about this document. Because I did, I loved it. I was a zealot. So, I called my mom. I asked her to send me the speech, and she had thrown it away. Which is weird because like most moms, she saves *everything*. When I was twelve, I got a buzz cut so I could look like Annie Lennox, and she still has the bag of hair. But for some reason she threw away my prize-winning speech. So I decided I would . . . resurrect the speech, and the contest, based on what I remember about myself at fifteen.

Here are a few things I remember: In addition to being terrifyingly turned on all the time, I had an active fantasy life that was . . . sinister . . . filled with violence and . . . well, violence. I was also obsessed with witches, and the Salem witch trials, theater (here I am!), and most importantly, Patrick Swayze.

(Heidi turns and walks through the frame and up onto the stage.)

This is the American Legion hall in Wenatchee, Washington. This is where I'm from: "The Apple Capital of the World." This hall is not—it's not a naturalistic representation. I got my friend Rachel to help me reconstruct it from my dreams. It's like one of those crime-victim drawings.

(She looks around, feeling slightly uncomfortable now.)

Also, I forgot a door.

(She discovers a book from her childhood in the room.)

Ah! This is the actual book I used to prepare for the contest: *Your Rugged Constitution.* It's fantastic. There are little cartoons that explain all the amendments to you. It's endorsed by Herbert Hoover! I noticed the other day that this copy was published in 1954, which means that it didn't have all the amendments, but that never stopped me from winning. Actually, I didn't lose very often because I was really fucking good at this contest. My fiercest competitor was this genius girl named Becky Lee Dobbler from Lawrence, Kansas, who gave a speech every year about how the Constitution was a patchwork quilt. The thing she was so good at, though, is that—well, in order to win this thing, you had to draw a personal connection between your own life and the document, and Becky was amazing at this. She would tell these incredible stories about her pioneer grandmother, who, I don't know, like ate people along the trail. This part was harder for me when I was fifteen. I was, uh, pretty emotionally guarded. And I didn't want to talk about my grandmother.

(A beat. Heidi really takes in the audience for a moment. She makes eye contact, maybe smiles at someone in particular, allows herself a moment to prepare for what's about to come.)

We performed these speeches to audiences of older—mostly white—men, and in my memory, they were all smoking cigars. I would love it if you would be the men for me. You are all men now. Thank you. *(Beat)* Okay, I'm going to start. I'm going to be fifteen, but I'm not going to do anything special to make myself fifteen. So here I am. I'm fifteen.

(Heidi sits in one of the "contestant" chairs. There is a subtle shift in the energy of the room. The sound of a door opening at the back of the house. The Legionnaire walks down the aisle and onto the stage. He is dressed in a blazer decked out with American Legion pins and wears a Legionnaire hat from LCW Legion Post Number Ten in Wenatchee. Now we really are in an American Legion hall in 1989.)

LEGIONNAIRE

Morning. Welcome to the regional finals of the American Legion Oratory Contest here at LCW Legion Post Number Ten in Wenatchee, Washington. This contest exists to develop a deeper appreciation for the U.S. Constitution among high school students and to help them pay for college. Since 1938, the American Legion has awarded over three million dollars in college scholarships. Past winners have included several politicians and genuine celebrities, including former presidential candidate Alan Keyes and *Moneyline* host Lou Dobbs.

Before we begin, I ask that you do not applaud until the contest is completed. We don't want you to sway the judges. I would also ask that you refrain from taking pictures or recording any video. It would be a good idea if you put your camera away now until the end of the contest so that there is no temptation to take a picture and also to prevent accidental picture-taking. I would also ask that anyone wearing an alarm-type watch or carrying a pager, to please deactivate it now. Except doctors. We may need you.

(He laughs. Regrets it.)

Also, please show these kids the respect of only smoking in between speeches. Here are the rules: This is a two-part contest. In Part One, the contestants will get seven minutes to deliver a prepared oration that demonstrates his or her understanding of the Constitution and draws a personal connection between their own lives and this great document. In Part Two, the contestants will draw an amendment from this can, right here in full view of the audience. They will not have time to prepare a speech. They will have to speak extemporaneously on this amendment.

This part of the contest is tough, and I'm not going to make it any easier on these kids. They're smart; they can take it. During their speeches, I may challenge them on certain points. I may not. We want to give them an idea of what it will be like when they're arguing in front of the Supreme Court one day.

Today's contestants are Becky Lee Dobbler from Lawrence, Kansas, who brings us: "The Constitution is a Patchwork Quilt." And Heidi Schreck from Wenatchee, Washington: "Casting Spells: The Crucible of the Constitution."

(He applauds for the kids and encourages the audience to join him.)

Let's give these kids a hand before the contest starts. Get it out of your systems.

(He lets them clap for a moment and then raises his hands to stop them.
 He turns to Heidi.)

Heidi Schreck.

(Heidi joins the Legionnaire center stage. They shake hands.)

Please approach the podium.

(She walks to the podium.)

Your time begins . . . now.

(The Legionnaire starts the stopwatch.)

HEIDI

The Constitution is a living document. That is what is so beautiful about it. It is a living, warm-blooded, steamy document. It is *not* a patchwork quilt. It is hot and sweaty. It is a crucible. Do you know what a crucible is? It is a . . . pot in which you put many different ingredients and boil them together until they transform into something else. Something that is sometimes magic. So you see, our Constitution is like a witch's cauldron.

Of course, you all know so much more about the Constitution than I do because you have all fought in wars. Thank you. Thank you for fighting for our country, and also for giving me so much scholarship money. Looking at all of you reminds me of a fantasy I used to have as a little girl. About being attacked by a rapist or murderer. A rapist or murderer who is a man. Like all of you. In my fantasy, I am able to convince the murderer and rapist not to murder me because I make you see that—just like you—I am a human being.

You say, "I'm here to murder you." And I say, "No. Think about this for a moment. Just like you, I am a human being." And then you see me for the first time as a human being and you say, "You're right! Oh my God, you are a human being!" And you start to cry and I forgive you and a rainbow appears, and we climb up on that rainbow together. And by this time a big crowd of my friends from school has gathered on the street below and they're so jealous to see me walking on that rainbow— "Doesn't she have to be in school? How can she be so special?" And I'm like, "I'm delivering this poor man to Heaven, have a good time in P.E."

How does this relate to the Crucible of the Constitution?

Well you see, a crucible is a witch's cauldron—that is one definition. But a crucible is also a severe test . . . of patience or belief. A severe test such as the one you and I went through when you wanted to murder me. Exactly like with our situation, the Constitution can be thought of as a boiling pot in which we are thrown together in sizzling and steamy conflict to find out what it is we truly believe.

This is why it's such a radical document. Two hundred and two years ago, a bunch of magicians came together during a sweltering summer day in Philadelphia, and they wanted to murder each other, but instead they sat down and performed a collective act of ethical visualization. Or as I like to call it: a spell.

Now did they get everything right? No. But that's what amendments are for, aren't they? And that's why to conclude my speech, I'd like to talk about the most magical and mysterious amendment of them all: Amendment 9.

Amendment 9 says: "The enumeration in the Constitution, of certain rights, shall not be construed to deny or disparage others retained by the people."

Do you know what this means? It means that just because a certain right is not listed in the Constitution, it doesn't mean you don't have that right. The fact is there was no possible way for the framers to put down every single right we have— the right to brush your teeth, sure you've got it, but how long do we want this document to be?

Here's another example: When I was a little girl, I had an imaginary friend named Reba McEntire. She was not related to the singer. Just because the Constitution does not proclaim the having of imaginary friends as a right, does not mean I can be thrown in jail for being friends with Reba McEntire. Isn't that amazing! Think about this for a second: The Constitution doesn't tell you all the rights that you have . . . because it doesn't *know*.

When the great Supreme Court Justice William O. Douglas talked about this amendment, he used the word "penumbra." What is a penumbra? Well, gentlemen, here I am standing in the light. And there you are, sitting in darkness. And this space between us . . . this space of partial illumination, this shadowy space right here: This is a penumbra.

People laughed at Douglas for calling it this but I like it. I think it's a helpful way to think about the Constitution and maybe even about our lives. Here we are, trapped between what we can see, and what we can't. *We* are stuck in a penumbra.

(The Legionnaire holds up a card that reads "Two Minutes." Heidi clocks this and moves quickly toward her conclusion.)

It's like how when I was a kid, I used to believe that I was a changeling. I mean, I still think I might be a changeling but I'm going to keep acting like a human being until my real family comes along to claim me. I would sit on the shores of Spirit Lake in the shadow of Mount St. Helens and wait for my real family—the swimming fairies—to grab me by the legs and drag me under the water. And we would swim down as deep as we could possibly go, and just when I was about to drown, we would pop up in another lake on the other side of the world. And when I stepped onto the shores of this new land, I would finally understand who I really was.

This is why I love Amendment 9 so much. It acknowledges that who we are now may not be who we will become. It leaves a little room . . . for the future self?

(The Legionnaire holds up a card that reads "Ten Seconds." Heidi rushes to finish her speech.)

And we just have to hope we don't drown in the process of figuring out what that is. Thank you.

(The Legionnaire rings the bell. If anyone applauds, he warns them to stop.)

LEGIONNAIRE

No applause please.

(He approaches her, carrying a coffee can.)

Now for the extemporaneous part of our contest! These kids have spent all year studying six different constitutional amendments. Today, they are going to pick one of them to speak about, right here, off the top of their heads. Miss Schreck, I am going to ask you to pick an amendment from this can.

HEIDI

(To the audience) I loved this part of the contest. The adrenaline. Trying to remember all the facts about the amendment. Also, my dad coached me on this part and it was nice because—well, I was fifteen, so we were having a really hard time and talking about the Constitution was a way for us both to pretend I wasn't becoming a woman.

(She looks back at the Legionnaire and draws an amendment. She reads it out loud:)

The 14th Amendment. Section 1.

LEGIONNAIRE

The 14th Amendment is big, folks. It contains four different sections that have changed the lives of every person in this room. Now, because 14 is such a bear, the contestant will only address Section 1 of this amendment. *(To Heidi)* You ready?

(Heidi recites the text of the 14th Amendment, Section 1, from memory, as if reenacting her long-ago practice sessions with her father.)

HEIDI

The 14th Amendment, Section 1: All persons born or naturalized in the United States, and subject to the jurisdiction thereof, are citizens of the United States and of the State in which they reside. No State shall make or enforce any law which shall abridge the privileges or immunities of citizens of the United States; nor shall any State deprive any person of life, liberty, or property, without due process of law; nor deny to any person within its jurisdiction the equal protection of the laws.

(The Legionnaire nods. Proud.)

LEGIONNAIRE

Well done. *(To the audience)* She will have one minute for her overview and two minutes to address each of the *four clauses* of the 14th Amendment, Section 1. And just a reminder: Make this as personal as possible. Tell us how this amendment has affected your life.

(The Legionnaire checks his watch.)

Your time begins now.

(Heidi launches in as quickly as possible in order to fit everything into the time limit.)

HEIDI

Okay. Okay. So the 14th Amendment is like a giant, supercharged force field protecting all of your human rights. It comes right after the 13th Amendment—which as you all know abolished slavery—ending the most shameful chapter in our nation's history. Lincoln knew though that just ending slavery would not be enough, so he got his friend John Bingham to help him write the 14th and 15th Amendments: The Reconstruction Amendments. These amendments made the newly freed slaves citizens, guaranteed them equal protection under the law, and protected their right to vote.

This amendment was a huge force in the Civil Rights movement. It facilitated the desegregation of schools, buses, and hospitals—although that would take almost a hundred years. And let's be clear, somebody had to activate the force field. It took the heroic work of Civil Rights leaders like Martin Luther King, Jr.; Dorothy Height; Rosa Parks; Bayard Rustin to rouse the great powers of Amendment 14.

I want to emphasize that this amendment guaranteed equal rights only to men. Black women were not given these rights. No women were given these rights. The question of Native American rights never even came up. Even Lincoln was trapped in a penumbra on that one.

This is the first time the word "male" is explicitly used in the Constitution. So, whereas before there was a little room for interpretation about whether women could vote, now it was explicit: We could not vote. Lincoln asked us to wait just a tiny bit longer to get the vote. Just like fifty-four years longer—

LEGIONNAIRE

Voting is outlined in Section 2. Please stick to Amendment 14, Section 1.

HEIDI

Right, sorry. Wonderful. *(To the audience)* My dad says this is what we call the penalty box of democracy. Sometimes you have to wait for things. Sometimes it's better to fix one bad thing than to try to fix two bad things and fail.

(The Legionnaire rings the bell. Heidi heads for the podium.)

LEGIONNAIRE

Clause 1: "Any persons born on U.S. soil—and subject to the jurisdiction thereof—are citizens of the United States." Your time begins now.

(Heidi thinks for a moment, and then launches in with confidence.)

HEIDI

Clause 1 overturned the most disgusting Supreme Court decision in history: *Dred Scott v. Sandford.*

Dred Scott was a slave who sued for his freedom in 1857 after living as a free man with his wife and daughters in Illinois. Not only did our Supreme Court decide that Dred Scott would have to remain a slave, they ruled that no person of African ancestry could ever become a United States citizen. Four members of this court owned slaves themselves.

(Heidi steps out from behind the podium.)

Although he lost, Dred Scott's brave action ignited the forces of abolition, led to Lincoln signing the Emancipation Proclamation, and ultimately enshrined in law right here in the 14th Amendment the right of every person born on U.S. soil to become a citizen, except Native Americans.

One other tricky thing about this clause is that it doesn't say anything about how immigrants can become citizens. It leaves it up to the whims of lawmakers to decide who they think is a "good" immigrant or a "bad" immigrant. For example, in 1882, the government decided Chinese immigrants were "dangerous" and "stealing jobs." So they passed the Chinese Exclusion Act, which made immigration from China illegal until 1943.

(The Legionnaire holds up a thirty-second card. Heidi clocks it, panicked.)

On a deeply personal note, my great-great-grandmother Theresa was considered a "good" immigrant. She came to Washington State from Gengenbach, Germany, in 1879, because my great-great-grandfather ordered her from a catalog! The reason she was considered a "good" immigrant is because at the time the male-to-female ratio in Washington State was 9 to 1.

(The Legionnaire holds up a ten-second card.)

I don't know if my great-great-grandmother wanted to come to America or not. I do know that she died at age thirty-six in a mental institution, and therefore she was never able to become a—

(The Legionnaire rings the bell.)

—citizen. Thank you!

(Disoriented, Heidi heads back to the podium and attempts to regroup.)

LEGIONNAIRE

Clause 2: "No State shall make or enforce any law which shall abridge the privileges or immunities of citizens of the United States." Your time begins now.

HEIDI

Clause 2 ensures that you, as Americans, are free to travel from State to State; free to buy property in any State; and free to pursue happiness in every State.

(Heidi pauses, gives sideways glance to the Legionnaire, then moves out from behind the podium, determined to somehow loop her speech back around to her great-great-grandmother.)

Here's a fascinating story . . . about interstate travel.

The lack of women during my great-great-grandmother's time was considered such a big problem in Washington State, that in 1865 a man named Asa Mercer cooked up a scheme to deliver five hundred women to Seattle.

He went back east to Lowell, Massachusetts, and told the women there—many of whom had been working in factories since they were seven years old—that Seattle was a paradise for ladies. The kind of place where they could live free and independent lives—become teachers, writers, milliners. Then he went back to Seattle and told the men if they gave him three hundred bucks, he could deliver them a bride.

Now, even with all this money, Mercer couldn't afford a boat. So, he wrote to Lincoln and asked for an old military ship to transport the women. Lincoln did not write back—it was 1865, he was busy. So Mercer hopped a train, took it all the way to DC to talk to Lincoln in person, only to arrive and discover the Capitol was wreathed in black, because Lincoln had just been assassinated.

Now you'd think this might have stopped Mercer's plan, but no. Instead, he went to Ulysses S. Grant and said he *had* talked to Lincoln—like a while back—and that Lincoln had promised him this boat. And yes, he was sad about Lincoln, but the boat? Grant said, "Take it."

A few days into the journey, the ship's crew began to spread rumors onboard that Seattle was *not* a paradise for ladies. The men there were loggers and drunks who beat up their wives. So, when the boat reached Chile, fifteen women demanded to get off the boat. Mercer said sure, they could deboard in the morning, and then in the middle of the night he pulled up anchor, effectively kidnapping them.

(The Legionnaire holds up a ten-second card. Heidi speeds up to get to the personal part.)

My great-great-grandmother was purchased for around seventy-five dollars when my great-great-grandfather ordered her from the *Matrimonial Times*—

LEGIONNAIRE

Clause 3.

(The Legionnaire rings the bell.)

HEIDI

(To Legionnaire) Uh wait, wait, hold on. *(To the audience)* Since I've been working on this I've been wondering about my great-great-grandmother. She died of melancholia. That was her official diagnosis: "Melancholia. Age thirty-six. Western State Mental Hospital." I also grew up believing that all the women in my family inherited chemical depres-

sion from Theresa and her melancholia. We all take various forms of medication for it—they're working! We also all cry in the same loud, melodramatic way. I like to call it "Greek Tragedy Crying." It's where no matter what happens to you, you howl and you wail as if—well, as if you've just killed your two sons because your husband betrayed you and it sounds like this:

(She wails. And wails. Very loudly. She recovers.)

I lost so many boyfriends this way. One of them told me the crying just felt too aggressive. It felt like I was crying "at him." Anyway, lately, I've been wondering about Theresa's diagnosis. There are no records of what her daily life was like, but it seems like it must have been really hard.

(Heidi slips some index cards from her pocket.)

These are some headlines I found in the *Cowlitz County Register*, her hometown newspaper. These events all happened in one week:

"Napavine Man Shoots Wife in Back"
"Husband Stomps Wife's Face with Spiked Logging Boots"
"Jealous Husband Ties Woman to Bed for Three Days"

And this one: "B. Phelps ran into her daughter's apartment to find her son-in-law in the act of shooting her fleeing daughter. 'Get out of here,' he said. 'Everything here belongs to me.'"

(The Legionnaire rings the bell.)

LEGIONNAIRE

Clause 3.

27

(Heidi looks at the Legionnaire. Really? She reluctantly returns to the podium.)

"Nor shall any State deprive any person of life, liberty, or property without due process of law." Your time begins now.

(Fifteen-year-old Heidi's face lights up. She loves this clause.)

HEIDI

This is one of the most miraculous clauses in our entire Constitution! The due process clause. We stole it from the Magna Carta. It ensures that the government cannot lock you up, take your stuff, or kill you—without a good reason. It is also the heart of the 1973 Supreme Court case *Roe v. Wade*, a case that's all about penumbras.

(Heidi checks in quickly with the Legionnaire and presses on.)

With the help of Justice William O. Douglas's beautiful penumbra metaphor, Justice Harry Blackmun used the 9th Amendment to shine a light into the other amendments, and he found there, in the shadows of the Constitution, the right to privacy and he declared that this gave a woman the right to decide what to do with her own body. Well, technically, he argued that a doctor and his patient have a right to privacy, so that he can decide what to do with her body.

This was a special moment for the 9th and 14th Amendments. They came together in a "Wonder Twin powers activate" kind of way to protect a woman's right to choose. Of course, depending on your view, gentlemen, you may consider this an unholy alliance. My view, which I feel obligated to share even if it endangers my scholarship money, is that I support a woman's right to choose. Although, it's a choice I would *never* make personally. *(To the audience)* I said that. I did, I said that in the contest. And then six years later I got pregnant, so that was confusing.

(She sneaks away from the Legionnaire to confide in the audience.)

I got pregnant while playing Miss Julie at a tiny theater in Seattle. I got pregnant by the actor playing Jean, obviously. We were performing on a double bill with a beautiful Maria Irene Fornes play called *Springtime*, which was a tender love story between two women and, in retrospect, I wish I had been cast in that play instead.

I didn't know what to do. I was twenty-one. I had just graduated college and I was back in Wenatchee living in my parents' basement. I was helping my dad paint houses for the summer so I could save up money to move to Siberia. I studied Russian in college, and I was going to teach English there for one million rubles a month. (Which, at that time, was about two hundred dollars, because we had just helped Russia destroy their economy with disaster capitalism, setting us up for the very situation we're in right now, but that's a whole other play. I will let you know when it's ready.)

I decided to take a pregnancy test, mostly because I was hoping it was one of those hysterical pregnancies like ladies in soap operas get. I couldn't go to Planned Parenthood though, because my mom's best friend worked there, and I couldn't buy a test at a drugstore because it's a small town, someone might see me and tell my parents. So I looked in the phone book, I found this listing that said "Free Pregnancy Testing. Quick. Confidential!" *(To the Legionnaire)* Sir, I'm gonna keep going.

I went downtown to Wenatchee Ave. I snuck in the back door of this unmarked building, and the first thing I saw when I walked inside is that the walls were covered with pictures of fetuses. I panicked. I wanted to run, but in case you can't tell by this point in the show, I was raised to be psychotically polite. So, when Marcy the receptionist smiled and told me how happy she was that I had come, I smiled back and said, "Me too."

Marcy took my hand. She said, "Heidi, if you are pregnant, will this be good news or bad news?" And I started to cry, loudly, but because I didn't want to disappoint Marcy, I said, "Good! Really good news!" And then she hugged me, and she smelled so good—she smelled just like my Grandma Betty, like White Shoulders perfume that's been left out in the sun a little too long.

My town was an abortion-free zone. You had to drive three hours west to Seattle or five hours east to Spokane to get an abortion. I decided to go eight hours south to Eugene, Oregon (using my right to travel from the privileges and immunities clause of the 14th Amendment), because there's a clinic there called the Feminist Women's Health Collective run by lesbians, and I thought that must be the best possible place on the planet to get an abortion.

And that's what I wanted. I wanted an abortion. I knew it was my right, I knew it was legal. I knew it had been technically legal for the first hundred years we were a country. Because I'd been able to go to college, I knew abortion hadn't become a crime until the late nineteenth century, right before the government started forcibly sterilizing women of color and indigenous women.

I knew that Gloria Steinem had had an abortion and Billie Jean King and Susan Sontag. I knew that Penny from *Dirty Dancing* had had an abortion. And I knew that when Jennifer Grey asked her dad, Jerry Orbach, to save Penny's life after her back-alley abortion almost killed her, I knew she was asking a lot of her dad because this was the 1960s and Jerry Orbach could have been arrested for getting anywhere near an abortion. And I knew that this is how we were supposed to understand that Jerry Orbach was a good man, and also how we knew that Jennifer Grey and Patrick Swayze's love was *real*.

That is everything that was going through my head while Marcy and I were hugging. I didn't say any of that to her though. She told me my test was positive. I said, "Thank you!" and headed for the door, and she followed me. She shoved a pamphlet in my hand that explained if I chose to have an abortion I would end up suicidal and barren, and then she tucked in the tag at the back of my dress. "I can't help myself," she said. "Always a mother."

I didn't tell my own mother what I was really thinking or feeling either. I didn't tell her I was pregnant. I don't know why. My mom's a feminist. She marched for the Equal Rights Amendment. She even had one of those white-lady feminist theater troupes that did puppet shows of like *The Yellow Wallpaper*, but for some reason I didn't feel like I could tell her. In fact, the only person I told for twenty-five years was Jean. He was so chivalrous. He offered to pay—for half of it—and he even suggested we drive down Highway 101 and camp on the beach to save money, make some kind of vacation out of it.

(Heidi checks in with the Legionnaire, suddenly self-conscious again.)

I shouldn't have to say this, but I was on birth control when I got pregnant. I had been on the pill since I was fifteen years old. My friend Renee and I snuck in the back door of Planned Parenthood before my mom's friend worked there. Neither of us were having sex yet, but we wanted to be on birth control in case we went in a hot tub and the sperm swam up and attacked us. Or, you know, in case of a real attack.

I remember it was such a nice day. We went to McDonald's and washed down our first pills with chocolate shakes, and I could kind of feel it working right away. I felt very womanly. I felt like something came alive inside of me.

(She might be inspired to do a womanly dance here.)

What I didn't know at the time was that birth control had been legal for all women in this country for just fifteen years. I mean, I was fifteen, so, I thought it had been legal since the dawn of time! But no, no, in 1965 this incredible woman, Estelle Griswold, got herself arrested for providing birth control to poor women at her Connecticut Planned Parenthood. She faced a year in prison, took her case all the way to the Supreme Court and this, *this* is when William O.

Douglas brought out his beautiful penumbra metaphor, and declared that one thing the Constitution surely contains is the right to privacy, and that this allows a woman to put in an IUD—as long as she is married and as long as her husband says that it is okay!

This was a such scary moment for William O. Douglas; he really put himself on the line for us! Because the truth is *nobody knows what the 9th Amendment means.* Justice Scalia said he didn't even remember studying it in law school. Scalia said he couldn't tell you what the 9th Amendment meant if his life depended on it—and I guess his didn't!

So poor William O. Douglas had to dig up this amendment that nobody really uses, nobody understands, because there was no other way to deal with a female body. Because our bodies, *our bodies,* had been left out of this Constitution from the beginning! The framers were just like, *(Deep "man's voice") "Er, er. We don't know . . ." (Patting her body) "We don't know what to do with this kind of a hrrrmph . . ." (Heidi finds a "man" in the front row and gives him a charming fifteen-year-old smile)* I'm sorry, sir, I know that you do not speak like that.

(She will not stop smiling.)

So he had to dig up this amendment that nobody understands because he *wanted* to make birth control legal. He wanted to because, well, because it turns out that William O. Douglas—who was sixty-seven years old—was having an affair with a twenty-two-year-old college student! And two other justices may have been having sex with young women as well. So, I'm thinking—right?—he needed to find a way to get the birth control flowing! *(Heidi looks up to the stage manager's booth)* Terri, can you?

Since we're out of time already, sir, *(She curtsies to the Legionnaire)* I'm gonna play you a snippet of the actual Supreme Court recordings, because the arguments are fascinating. Trenchant. Remember it's 1965. There will not be a woman on this court until Sandra Day O'Connor arrives in 1981. So, here are nine men deciding the fate of birth control. Three of whom may have been cheating on their wives.

(Terri plays a recording from the Griswold v. Connecticut *Supreme Court hearing in 1965.*

Heidi stands and listens, trying to parse the arguments as if hearing them for the first time. She may sneak a few glances at the Legionnaire as it plays.)

JUSTICE POTTER STEWART

(Voice-over) Now that I've interrupted you, you've told us that in Connecticut the sale of uh . . . these devices is uh . . . not molested because they're sold for the prevention of disease. Is this uh . . . true about all of these devices that are covered uh . . . that each of them has the potential dual function of acting in a contraceptive capacity and as a prevention of disease, or only with respect to some of them?

WILLIAM I. EMERSON

(Voice-over) It's probably only true with respect to some, but some get by under the term "feminine hygiene," and uh . . . others uh . . . *(Cough)* uh . . . *(Cough)* uh . . . I—I—I just don't know about, but uh *(Cough)* uh . . . *(Cough)* They are, they are all sold in Connecticut drug stores on one theory or another.

JUSTICE EARL WARREN

(Voice-over) Is there anything in the record to *(Cough)* to indicate uh . . . *(Cough)* the uh, stem of the birth rate in Connecticut vis-à-vis the States that don't have such laws?

(The recording ends.)

HEIDI

It's like four hours of that.

(A beat. She might move closer to the audience.)

Birth control became legal for single women in 1972, the year after my mom got pregnant with me. *(The Legionnaire coughs)* This is what I was thinking about when my mom drove me to Seattle to meet Jean for our vacation, which is what I told her I was doing. I was thinking about the fact that she was my age when she had me, that she had dreamed of moving to New York to become an actor and a writer (which is of course what I'm going to do, but I don't know that yet), and as soon as I have that thought, I'm overcome by a sudden wave of nausea. I ask her to pull the car over. I open the door, I puke on the side of the road, and when I sit back up, I can tell that she knows.

And I'm waiting for her to tell me that it's okay—that it's my body, and like she taught me this is my decision. But when I look at my mom, she has this wild look in her eyes and then she starts hyperventilating, she's having some kind of panic attack. And suddenly she shouts: "You better not be pregnant!" And I shout: "I'M NOT PREGNANT!"

(The Legionnaire rings the bell.)

Clause 4!

(Heidi returns to the podium.)

LEGIONNAIRE

"No State shall deny to any person within its jurisdiction the equal protection of the laws."

HEIDI

Clause 4 is even more miraculous than Clause 3. The equal protection clause. It says that we all must be treated equally, that we cannot be discriminated against on the basis of race, sex, religion, or immigration status. It actually uses the word "person," not "citizen." Which means that if you are an undocumented immigrant, you must be given all the protections of Clause 3, the due process clause. You cannot be locked up without a fair trial. You cannot have anything—or anyone—seized from you—

(Heidi drops the fifteen year old's smile.)

I've been talking about this clause for a long time. And I find it harder and harder to talk about every day. Also, uh, I do have a personal connection to this clause, but I never would have talked about it at fifteen. I didn't tell *anyone*. And whenever I get to this part, I have a desire to protect my fifteen-year-old self from talking about it.

(She starts to take off her sunny yellow blazer.)

So I'm going to talk about the equal protection clause as myself, now. In fact, I'm just gonna go ahead and be myself all the time now.

(She lays her blazer carefully on the chair. She returns to the podium.)

. . . a grown woman in my mid-forties. Hello. Also my face just fucking hurts from smiling. *(She turns to the Legionnaire)* I'm not sure what your purpose is anymore, sir.

(The Legionnaire is not sure either. Heidi releases any last remnants of the buoyant, performative girlishness that is one of her lifelong coping mechanisms.)

The equal protection clause really is miraculous. People have used it to do so much good in this country. It was the heart of the Civil Rights Act. Twenty-six years after this contest, it will be used to make same-sex marriage possible. It was used to win all sorts of rights for working women, including the right to equal pay and the right to be free from sexual harassment.

A few years after the contest, lawyers tried to use the equal protection clause to address the problem of sexual and physical violence toward women. The idea being that a person can't possibly be considered equal if they are subject to epidemic levels of gender-based violence.

As you may already know, and if you don't know, you should read more: Four women are murdered every day in this country by a male partner. One in four girls will be sexually abused before they turn eighteen. One in four women will be raped by the time they are my age now. And ten million American women live in violent households.

[These numbers are based on published statistics from the National Sexual Violence Resource Center in the year 2019. They should be updated in performance to reflect the current reality.]

My mom lived in a house like this. So did my Grandma Betty. And most likely my great-great-grandma Theresa—though there isn't any evidence of this, except maybe, *maybe* the fact that she died of melancholia at age thirty-six.

(Heidi turns to the Legionnaire.)

Will you hand me my Grandma Betty index cards?

(Heidi walks to the Legionnaire as he finds the index cards. She takes them and shuffles through them.)

I know this story well but I prefer to read it.

(She begins to read from the cards. Each paragraph is written on a separate card.)

My Grandma Betty married my grandpa when she was nineteen. He was what we call in my family a "good man," meaning he didn't beat up his wife and kids.

He was a six-foot-six logger who built the one-bedroom house they lived in with his bare hands. Legend has it he chopped down the trees to build her a house, and then he dragged the lumber up from the base of Mount St. Helens on his back like a horse. (I've never understood why, because he had a truck, but that's the story.)

Grandma Betty and her good husband had two kids when my grandma got pregnant with my mom. One day she was feeling antsy and she wanted to go to the Cowlitz County Fair. My grandpa took an extra logging shift to pay for the tickets. He and his partner Ray were sawing a hundred-and-fifty-foot evergreen tree. They misjudged the trajectory of the tree and it fell on my grandpa, killing him.

My mom was born while my grandma was still grieving.

My widowed Grandma Betty supported her three kids by working as a waitress at the local diner. A young barber came in often. He was very good-looking. My grandma loved good-looking men. As do I. My grandma married the barber pretty quickly and pretty quickly he started to beat her up. He beat up her kids. They had three more kids together. He beat them up, too.

When my mom's sister turned sixteen, my grandma's husband raped her. She got pregnant and went away to have the baby. He raped her again. She went away again. She came back home after giving birth to a second child, and graduated at the top of her class—

By the way, all of these kids grew up to be pretty happy. They grew up to be kind and loving people. They all have families that they adore and jobs that, like most of us, they kind of like. None of them perpetuated the abuse that had been inflicted on them. I realize it's not great storytelling to skip to the end like that, but I don't want you to have to worry about them for the rest of the show. They are okay. Like so many people in this country who go through similar things—and there are so many people who do—they are mostly okay—

(The Legionnaire takes the index cards from Heidi's hands without being summoned and returns them to their place. He now seems to be transforming into her ally and assistant.)

I was so pissed off at my mom when she told me this story. She told me when I was fifteen and I was—I was *furious* with her because I was a deeply heterosexual fifteen-year-old girl. I wanted to make out with boys, like all the time! I did not want to think they could be violent. I mean sure, yes, they could be troubled. I loved it when they were troubled. They could be a . . . down-and-out dance instructor at a Catskills resort.

The thing I remember saying to my mom, though, is: "Why didn't Grandma just take all of you and run away?" My mom had no answer, she went into her room and shut the door and wouldn't come out, but my dad took me aside and explained that Grandma was sick. That she had this thing women get called "Battered Woman Syndrome." Which—I was so confused by this. Like, "Oh no, how do you catch that?" And also, if you'd ever met my Grandma Betty you'd know this was an absurd way to describe her. She was almost six feet tall. Half-German, half-Swede. Beautiful. Big muscles. Wild black hair. In addition to waitressing, her other jobs included *log runner*— that is where you stand on a bunch of logs in a raging river . . .

(Heidi begins to enact this.)

. . . and you take this giant stick and then you push logs down the river, all day, until they—I have no idea where the logs go.

(If she's having a good time, Heidi might keep log-rolling for a bit before she finally gets back to her story. She might say, "This is my favorite thing to do in the whole play!" And, pointing to the Legionnaire, "He can't stop me because I didn't write anything for him!")

This was not my grandma's dream job! What she really wanted to be was a painter. She, um, she taught herself to paint by copying Picasso, who was her favorite, so her one-bedroom house was covered with all of these . . . shitty-looking Picasso reproductions, and when I was a little girl, I thought they were her paintings. It wasn't until high school that I realized Picasso, not my grandma, had painted *The Weeping Woman.*

Whenever I think about the things the women in my family wanted to be, I get this weird pain in my back, and my throat squeezes up, like I can't get my voice out, and I guess I have this intense feeling of survivor's guilt.

It's funny—Jean and I stopped to visit my grandma on the way to my abortion, and I wanted to tell her what I was doing because I thought she might be happy for me. My great-grandma had sixteen children, my grandma had six children and a violent husband. I was the first generation in my family for whom childbirth was not obligatory, not mandated by the government. After the way my mom reacted, though . . .

We were sitting at the breakfast table eating these beautiful popovers she had made for us and I wanted to say: "Grandma

Betty, I'm pregnant!" And instead I said: "Grandma Betty, I miss George!" I don't know why I said that. George was this sock monkey she sewed when I was three years old. I loved this sock monkey to death. Truly, I murdered him with my love. He was missing an eye, he was missing a tail. Eventually, I had to put him in a little monkey coffin.

I told my grandma that I wished I still had George so I could take him to Siberia with me. She went: "Hm!" because she was very unsentimental. But the following Christmas she sewed me a brand-new sock monkey and she sent him all the way to Siberia. And I named this new sock monkey George the Second! And then when I turned forty, I decided George the Second was lonely and I bought him a friend: a tiny red-and-white-striped monkey I named George the Second's Friend. And to this day—I am married—George the Second's Friend is the most important person in my life. (You probably think I've gone off on a tangent. I haven't. There are no tangents in this show. In spite of how it feels, and apparently what some people think, this play is quite carefully constructed.)

(She stalks over to the Legionnaire, who is standing and ready to hand her the next set of index cards. He has now transformed into her assistant.)

In 2005, the due process clause of the 14th Amendment was invoked in a case called *Castle Rock v. Gonzales.* Jessica Gonzales obtained a permanent restraining order against her violent husband. A month later, he kidnapped their three daughters. Jessica, terrified, called the police seven times and went to the station twice in person to beg them to look for her daughters. The police not only refused to help Jessica, they told her to stop bothering them.

By morning, Mr. Gonzales had legally purchased a gun while their daughters waited in the car, and then killed them.

Jessica Gonzales—who now goes by her original name, Lenahan—Jessica Lenahan very bravely sued the Castle Rock Police Department for failing to show up to protect her and her kids. The State of Colorado had recently passed a law that required police to arrest a person for violating a restraining order. So Jessica sued, she won, and then the city appealed, took the case all the way to the Supreme Court. And this court, led by Antonin Scalia, overturned her case, killed the Colorado law, and gutted the Violence Against Women Act by ruling that the police had no constitutional obligation to protect Jessica or her daughters.

I've listened to this case so many times and the thing I noticed is that the justices spend very little time talking about Jessica as a human being. They don't talk about her daughters. Rebecca, who was ten; Katheryn, who was eight; Leslie, who was seven. Instead, they spend a long time arguing about the word "shall." As in the phrase "the police shall enforce a restraining order."

At one point, Justice Scalia and Justice Breyer got into a little discussion about whether either of them understood what the word "shall" *meant.* *(She looks up to the booth)* Terri, will you . . . ?

(Terri plays a clip of the justices debating the definition of the word "shall":)

JUSTICE ANTONIN SCALIA

(Voice-over) Wait wait, I thought we were just talking here about State law as to whether "shall" means "shall." Do you think that it's a matter of State law whether—whether, if it does mean "shall" it creates a property interest for purposes of the federal, uh, Constitution?

JOHN C. EASTMAN

(Voice-over) No, Justice Scalia, I don't—

JUSTICE STEPHEN BREYER

(Voice-over) Suppose "shall" does mean "shall." Fine. But you might have a statute that says the fire department shall respond to fires. And the police department shall respond to crimes. The army shall respond to . . . uh uh uh attacks. Even the word "shall" doesn't necessarily mean . . .

HEIDI

Scalia ultimately decided that "shall" did not mean "must." Which is confusing because Scalia was a devout Catholic. Feminist legal scholars have called this decision the death of the 14th Amendment for women. This ruling is most devastating for Black women, women of color, trans women, binary, and nonbinary trans folx, women with disabilities, immigrants—people who are less likely to be helped by police than I am. It's especially devastating to indigenous women, who suffer the most violence in our country.

(She thinks for a moment. She is grappling with a problem in real time, trying to find a way to connect feeling to thought.)

I really wanted to know why they decided this—maybe because of my family history of this kind of violence, I needed to understand it. So, I talked to a few constitutional scholars and this is what I learned.

I learned about two kinds of rights: negative rights and positive rights. Negative rights protect us from the government taking our stuff, locking us up, killing us. Positive rights are active rights.

They include things like the right to a fair trial, the right to counsel, in some countries the right to health care. Our Constitution, with some exceptions, is a negative-rights document, and Scalia, an originalist, was adamantly a negative-rights kind of guy, which is in part why he decided that Jessica Gonzales was not entitled to any active protection from the police. I also learned that if the Equal Rights Amendment had been ratified, she might have been protected under that. And I understood for the first time why my mom cried when it didn't pass.

So, what I'm trying to understand now is . . .

(Heidi searches for a way to articulate something.)

What does it mean if this document offers no protection against the violence of men? Sorry, I don't mean to—I have no desire to vilify men. I love men. I do. I fucking love you. I'm the daughter of a father! But the facts are extreme. Here's one statistic, just one: Since the year 2000, more American women have been killed by their male partners than Americans have died in the war on terror—including 9/11. That is not the number of women who have been killed by men in this country; that is only the number of women who have been killed by the men who supposedly love them.

That's such a staggering figure that I just kind of have to . . .
forget it, to get through the day. Except, I think you can't
forget about it. Even if you don't know the statistics, I think
you can feel the truth of that underneath everything . . .
humming. *(Unsure)* Right?

*(She looks to the Legionnaire for confirmation. He gives her
no response. She approaches him and talks directly to him for
the first time.)*

When I was seventeen, I used the money from your contest to go to college. I registered pre-law. I also auditioned
for the fall play, *Red Noses*. It was about a medieval theater
troupe trying to survive the plague. I played a one-legged
tap dancer who dies. At the first rehearsal this senior boy
asked me if I wanted a ride home and I said sure, and as
soon as we got to my dorm he said: "I've been wanting to
kiss you for so long," which was weird because we'd known
each other for three hours, but he was cute so I kissed him,
and then suddenly he took off my pants.

I was really smart when I was seventeen. I was! I was way
smarter than I am now. Plus, I had read everything—I
thought. I had read Audre Lorde and Gloria Steinem and
bell hooks. I was taking Advanced Feminist Studies. And
yet I just decided to go ahead and have sex with this guy
because it seemed like the polite thing to do, I think.

Or maybe . . . Now, I don't know.

When I think back about being in the car, I remember how
dark it was outside. I remember there was nobody on the
street, my dorm was way, way out on the edge of campus.
I remember having this kind of sick feeling in the pit of my

stomach and then this fleeting thought—so quick, I almost can't put it into language. But if I had to say it out loud, it would sound something like "stay alive."

Which is . . . It's strange because this guy would not have hurt me. I know he wouldn't. We're friends to this day. Well, we're Facebook friends. I'm ninety-nine-percent sure he would not have hurt me, so why did I feel like my life was in danger?

(Heidi turns to the Legionnaire.)

Could you read those Hammurabi index cards?

(The Legionnaire stands. He reads the cards:)

LEGIONNAIRE

- The first law pertaining to domestic violence comes from Hammurabi in 1800 B.C. It decreed that a husband could inflict punishment on any member of his household for any reason.
- The Roman Code of Paterfamilias said a man could kill his wife for adultery or for walking outside without her face covered.
- In Renaissance France, when it became clear that too many women and children were being beaten to death, and it was hurting the economy, men were restricted to blows that did not leave marks.
- In eighteenth-century England, the law said that a man could only hit his wife with a whip or stick no thicker than his thumb. Although many people think this is where the phrase "rule of thumb" originated, that's not actually true.

(Heidi interrupts. She moves to stand next to the Legionnaire, as if they are the father and daughter from American Gothic.*)*

HEIDI

Remember that thing I said about the male-to-female ratio in Washington State being 9 to 1? That's not true. That's what my history teacher Mr. Berger taught me. There were thousands of women in Washington, of course: the women of the Wenatchi tribes, the Salish tribes. And, apparently, some of these women had been marrying white men for a long time, and according to these women's journals, some of these marriages were actually good! Because these tribes were egalitarian. Women could be priests, translators, boat makers. Then Washington became a State and was under the umbrella of the Constitution (that I worshipped), which meant indigenous women were no longer considered people, the marriages became illegal, and they brought in a bunch of white women like my great-great-grandma Theresa. *(To the Legionnaire)* Go ahead.

LEGIONNAIRE

- In 1910, the U.S. Supreme Court ruled that a wife could not press assault charges against a husband, because it would open the doors of the courts to accusations of all sorts of one spouse against the other.
- In 1977, the California Penal Code stated that wives charging husbands with criminal assault must suffer more injuries than commonly needed for charges of battery.
- In 2005, the Supreme Court ruled that Jessica Lenahan could not sue the Castle Rock Police Depart-

ment for failing to show up to protect her and her children.

- In 2011, the Inter-American Commission on Human Rights ruled that the United States violated the human rights of Jessica Lenahan and her daughters.

HEIDI

Thank you, Mike. Everybody, this is Mike Iveson. Mike is a wonderful actor, a wonderful man, and . . . When I realized that there was going to be so much violence in this play, I really wanted some positive male energy up here with me.

(She turns to him. He looks a bit confused. Then he begins to speak. As he tells his story, he starts to remove his Legionnaire accoutrements: jacket, hat, tie. He is now Mike.)

MIKE

I'm representing a real person from Heidi's life, Mel Yonkin, who was a Legionnaire. Fought in World War II. He was an incredibly sweet man who would travel around the country with Heidi and her family from contest to contest. He always told her how proud he was of her, and when she won he would get kinda . . . misty. Pretend he had a cold.

I was very excited that Heidi asked me to be in the show, though I did think it was like a serious responsibility to be representing "positive male energy." I feel like I spent so many years refusing to be boxed in gender-wise, and I guess I thought of myself as having "gender-neutral" energy? Which, given that I always present myself as male, just seems sorta irresponsibly privileged to me sometimes.

Also, I would like to be able to report that I too had a crush on Patrick Swayze when I was younger like Heidi did, but the truth is I was kind of more into Mel Gibson. Yeah. I remember really wanting to be him in that movie *The Road Warrior*. After the movie came out I was always talking to my friends about: *(Bad Australian accent)* "Oh I'm gonna dye this little tuft of my hair blond over my ear," like Mel had in the movie. I thought I had a hilarious Australian accent, but you just heard it, it's a Cockney accent.

Which is interesting because my dad is a British working-class immigrant, but he's not a Cockney, he's from Wales and Yorkshire, which are two totally different accents, and I'm not going to do them and you *are* welcome. My dad is an incredibly charming guy, all my friends are really crazy about him and I remember when I was a kid both admiring his, like, masculine charisma, and also knowing that something about it was like a little put on?

For example, he went through a CB-radio phase. I was in high school, we were driving across country together, but we were in two separate cars, and he wanted us to stay in touch via CB radios. My dad would say stuff like, "Heads up, Mike, we're gonna take a left at the next exit," and I would say stuff like, "Hey, Dad, when are we going to get a bathroom break?" And one time another guy's voice busted in: "Coupla queers on the line." Some trucker or somebody— definitely a deep male voice, probably deeper than mine or my dad's. There was a terrible pause and a kind of pit in my stomach. Was my dad, like, lisping inadvertently? Or was I? Or something? And then my dad responded: "And a faggot listening in!" Which, all things considered, good save? I must not have been out to my dad at that point. There's no way he would've used that kind of language if he'd known I was gay back then.

I mean I didn't think I was gay back then either. Maybe I thought of my sexual orientation as "nerd." A couple years after that, I was in college, and I was going to drive from Maine to Boston to live with my girlfriend. I was still dating women at the time. And I was wearing a YSL slate-blue suit vest as a shirt; tight cotton cutoffs with big red, white, and blue stripes on them; and brown ankle boots with thick pink socks kind of peeking out the top. My dad saw me as I was walking out the door and he said: "You look ridiculous. You cannot wear this." I know he was just trying to protect me.

And maybe he had a point because a couple years after that, when I was first living in New York City, I was with four of my friends, I was walking from the Tunnel Bar to a bar that was just called The Bar, that was in the East Village. I was wearing black spandex Patricia Field hot pants with these little red velvet polka dots. And we passed a group of teenagers, and one of them punched me in the face.

As I've gotten older, I've become more comfortable just presenting as basic male. It feels, I don't know, more "me." I think?

A couple years ago, I was in Baltimore and I was at a sports bar called Pickles Pub. There was a guy at the bar—like six foot two, two hundred and thirty pounds, big, bald, white dude. The woman behind the bar was running around taking orders, he turns to me and says, "Don't you want to fuck her?"

There was a weird moment where I just didn't know how to respond. Was he really asking me? Because . . . I'm dressed like the kind of guy you ask that question to? Was he testing me to see if I was gay? Was he capable of violence? *(To Heidi)* Was that woman feeling like how you felt with the guy in the car that time? This guy was a beast physically, but I also had this weird sympathy for him. So, I slapped him on the back and said, "Good luck, man." And then I walked out of the bar.

(He looks to Heidi. She looks around at the American Legion hall.)

HEIDI

I'd really like for all of this to disappear now. This contest. All of . . . this. I wish we could have one of those spectacular set changes now, but uh—well, it's not that kind of play. So maybe we could all just imagine that we're somewhere else. Maybe we could imagine *something* else. And you are welcome to be yourselves again. You are so welcome to be yourself.

(Heidi gives the audience a few beats of silence to imagine something new.)

My mom and my aunt are the ones who reported their stepfather to the police, when they were teenage girls, because my Grandma Betty was too scared to do it. They had been born a little farther out of the penumbra than my grandma. They were born a little over twenty years after women had the right to vote.

When my mom's stepfather found out he'd been reported, he got his constitutionally protected gun, rounded up his family, and threatened to kill them all. And my Grandma Betty finally decided—in spite of the fact that she'd inherited the pretty logical belief that her life did not matter in the eyes of the law—in spite of that, she decided to take her children and run away.

The police showed up for my family. It was a small town. They were white. They arrested my mom's stepfather, but my grandma was too scared to testify against him, so my mom and my aunt did that too, when they were teenage girls. Their stepfather was sentenced to thirty years in prison. He served two. But the fact that he went to prison at all is probably why I get to be here right now, telling you these stories.

When I think about how brave my mom and my aunt were as teenage girls, well, it gives me such respect for them, but it also makes me think about the fact that progress doesn't only move one way. I've learned so much from younger people. You all seem braver than I remember being when I was your age, more compassionate. You certainly have a more sophisticated understanding of gender. Sometimes, I feel like you're shining a light backwards into the darkness so I can follow you into the future.

I've struggled my whole life to forgive my grandmother for not protecting my mom. I don't know if I can forgive her. But it's also confusing because I loved her so much. We all loved her. My mom loved her. My aunts and uncles loved her. And the Grandma Betty who didn't protect her kids is not the Grandma Betty I knew. The grandma I knew loved us all like crazy. She gave her whole life to her kids, her grand-kids, her great-grandkids. She sent me that sock monkey all the way to Siberia. She would have thrown her body in front of a truck for me! So I don't know how to make sense of my two grandmothers. Except while I've been making this, I've realized how many of us are forced to be two people in this culture.

I learned something from a younger person recently, a younger feminist, that helps me understand my grandma a little bit better. They taught me about this concept called "covert resistance." Covert resistance is the idea that seemingly passive, victim-like behaviors, people-pleasing behaviors, may actually be the sanest response to living in a violent culture. A culture, and a country, that is making it clear every single day, it has no interest in pro-tecting you.

In the case of my grandma, covert resistance is all the invisible, brave actions a woman takes inside a violent relationship she can't leave because she doesn't make as much money as a man; because the police might not show up when she calls; or if they do show up, depending on the color of her skin, something terrible might happen; because she doesn't have decision-making power over her own body.

Covert resistance doesn't fit into our traditional narratives of heroism. It involves a lot of tiny, daily actions—like a woman feeding her kids, hiding money away for them, mak-ing sure they get a good education (helping them graduate at the top of their class).

It can also include getting sick, maybe dying of melancholia, not leaving. Because in this country, the moment a woman tries to leave is the moment her life and her kids' lives are in the most danger.

When my Grandma Betty died, my uncle found thirty thousand dollars hidden under her mattress with a note that said to give five thousand dollars to each of her kids. She had been saving it for fifty years.

(She looks to Mike. She decides to shift gears.)

I took George the Second's Friend with me on a business trip to Los Angeles recently. He loves the West Coast. He was in my bag, wrapped up in a wool stocking cap to protect him. Then it got cold on the plane, so I took him out, put on the stocking cap, and hid him in an airplane blanket, so I wouldn't be, like, a middle-aged lady with a stuffed monkey on my lap.

Then suddenly I was at baggage claim and I realized I had left George the Second's Friend on the plane.

I don't even know how to— The only way to describe my reaction is to say that if Meryl Streep and I had been at the audition for that "dingo ate my baby" movie together, I would have gotten the part. I was WAILING. SOBBING. I was doing the Greek Tragedy Crying! I ran up to the help desk and the woman took one look at me: "Are you okay?" And I said: *(Wailing)* "NO. NO. I LEFT SOMETHING VERY VALUABLE ON THE PLANE." And she was like: "What is it?" And I said: "MY CHILD'S FAVORITE TOY." It gets worse: "AND MY CHILD IS VERY SICK."

I know! I know—but she really leapt into action! She called up to the gate: "GET THAT MONKEY OFF THE PLANE!" And then she swiped me through security, and I started running, faster than I've ever run in my entire life. I ran past like fourteen Starbucks. And when I got to the gate I could see George the Second's Friend just sitting happily on this guy's counter, so I ran up, tears still streaming down my face, but this guy paid no attention to me, so I was just like FUCK IT! and I grabbed George the Second's Friend, and collapsed onto the airport floor and kept wailing and wailing and wailing. And I have no idea what I was crying about. I don't know if I was crying for my Grandma Betty, or because of chemical depression, or because he's such a cute little monkey, or because of centuries and centuries of fucking inherited trauma, or maybe, maybe IT'S JUST THE APPROPRIATE RESPONSE TO EVERYTHING RIGHT NOW.

My mom says when you are paralyzed by rage and despair, you have to imagine a woman running along a beach with a dog. (There's more.) If you watch the dog it keeps running ahead and then running back, so it seems like progress is constantly being undone. But if you watch the woman, you can see that she is moving steadily forward and forward and forward . . . I hope?

I told my mom about my abortion recently because—well, I had to because I was gonna tell you all. She was so blasé about it. I was like, "Why did you freak out back then?" She said, "I can be calm about it now that I know your life turned out okay." She wanted to know if I was angry with her. I was like, "No, because my life turned out okay."

I think there were two mothers in the car with me that day. There's the first mother, who's a feminist, who made me do this contest so I could go to college, who ended the legacy of violent men in our family by testifying, at fifteen. And then there's the second mother, the mother who'd been terrorized as a child, the mother whose first memory at age three was seeing her stepfather punch her mother and thinking, "Oh no, this is what life is like." (And it is what life is like.) The mother who'd inherited centuries of belief in her own worthlessness.

No, not just belief: centuries of laws that explicitly told her she was worthless.

For me though, that first mother was enough. She taught me what my rights were, she taught me which laws were there to protect me—and I had laws to protect me at that time— I didn't need the second mother to be there for me in the moment, because I had laws.

Which just makes me think: Maybe we shouldn't think of the Constitution as a crucible, in which we're all fighting it out together, in which we go in front of a court of nine people to negotiate for our basic human rights, which is what we have been doing for two hundred and thirty years. Because if this is a battle, or even a negotiation, then the people who have always been in power, always dominated, always oppressed—men, white people—will continue to dominate and oppress. Maybe we could think of the Constitution like that first mother, a Constitution that is obligated to actively look out for all of us.

There are so many countries that have created modern, "positive rights" constitutions. Constitutions that actively protect human rights, guarantee health care, have provisions to protect the environment. One hundred and seventy-nine constitutions have explicit gender protections written into them. Ours is not one of them.

Our Constitution is *so old.*

Of course, the problem with making an all new "positive rights" Constitution is that we'd still have to trust the people interpreting those, right? We'd still have to trust the people who are in charge.

(Terri plays a recording of Ruth Bader Ginsburg's voice. Heidi puts her jacket back on and steps out of the frame.)

JUSTICE RUTH BADER GINSBURG

(Voice-over) The excuse for not hiring women in the criminal division was . . . they have to deal with all these tough types and . . . women aren't up to that. And I was amazed. I said: "Have you seen the lawyers at Legal Aid who are representing these tough types? They are women." People ask me sometimes: "When . . . when do you think it will be enough? When will it—will there be enough women on the Court?" And my answer is: "When there are nine."

PART TWO: THE DEBATE

Heidi steps out of the diorama and looks back at the American Legion hall.

HEIDI

I loved this contest. It made me believe that people would listen to me when I spoke. Also, I was fifteen: I had braces and horrible acne and it was nice to be valued for my brain.

While I was working on this re-creation, I met with young women who are doing these kinds of contests today.

(The shadow of a teenage girl appears along the back wall.)

I wanted to find out what they are thinking about the Constitution. About our country. And I invited one of these brilliant young women to join us here tonight.

(Rosdely Ciprian, fifteen, now stands where Heidi stood at the beginning of the show.)

ROSDELY

Hi. My name is Rosdely Ciprian. I'm a fifteen-year-old debater from New York City. I've been involved in parliamentary debate since the second semester of sixth grade. I've argued topics such as legalizing marijuana and whether the federal government should ban plastic bags. I have also spent the last year debating constitutional questions for audiences across the country, which is why Heidi invited me here tonight: to dig deeper into a big question about our founding document. Is it protecting us, or is it the source of our problems?

Personally I think the answer is both, but for the sake of having a good debate, we are each going to take a different side here tonight.

Before I explain to you the rules of parliamentary debate, though, let me say that the Constitution is *not* a crucible. At least that's not how I like to think of it. Why not just think of the Constitution as a human being? I mean, it was made by human beings so it's not a big stretch, right? Are human beings perfect? No. Are we capable of perfection? No. But that doesn't mean we are not valuable. We are always growing and changing. Learning. Just like us, this document is flawed. But just like us, it is also capable of getting better.

My opponent brought up the 9th Amendment in her prepared speech, which went *way* over time by the way. Sure, the penumbra metaphor is an interesting way to understand the 9th Amendment, and I am not arguing against it. But let me help you understand it another way:

I don't have any imaginary friends. But when I was younger, I did invent a fictional character named Boxellia. Boxellia is a scrillion-year-old AI robot who is shaped like a box and is much smarter than Siri because she knows everything, including the future. Boxellia knows what you're going to do next summer and she knows what life on Earth will be like a thousand years from now. To me, the 9th Amendment is like Boxellia. She holds the memory of our future. Too bad for us, we won't know what that is until we get there.

(To Heidi) Okay, let's start this debate!

(Heidi joins Rosdely center stage.)

HEIDI

For the past few years, Rosdely and I have been debating some of the questions that have come up tonight and, like she said, we are going to have a real, live debate for you, right here, right now.

ROSDELY

Our topic is: "Should We Abolish the United States Constitution?"

(The ushers pass out pocket Constitutions to the audience during the following exchange. There should be one pocket Constitution for each audience member.)

HEIDI

And there are some amazing folks passing out pocket Constitutions for you, so you can follow along, check our work.

ROSDELY

Usually there are three people on a team, but we are going to do this one-on-one tonight. This is a style I like to call "Iron Woman." Typically, in parliamentary debate we use a form called PO-POOP which is "Proposition, opposition-proposition, opposition, opposition, proposition," but we've made up a special style that we are calling POPOPO: "Proposition, opposition, proposition, opposition, proposition, opposition."

MIKE

The debaters have been training me to be the moderator and my most important duty is to flip a coin to determine which side of the argument our debaters will take. Rosdely, please call it in the air.

(Mike flips a coin. Rosdely and Heidi call out heads or tails. Mike turns to the person who wins the coin toss.)

[Note: Rosdely and Heidi have developed their arguments through years of debating extemporaneously together, and portions of this debate change from night to night. The following is a transcript from a preview performance at New York Theatre Workshop in New York City in September 2018.]

Heads it is, which side would you like to take?

ROSDELY

Uh . . . ? Opposition: "Keep."

HEIDI

Proposition: "Abolish."

MIKE

Okay. Debaters, you have ninety seconds to prepare. Starting now.

(Heidi and Rosdely rush to sit at two card tables that Mike has set up for them. The tables are covered with index cards, legal pads, pens, highlighters, water, and other supplies they might need. They prepare in silence, writing their points on index cards, etc.)

Rosdely has also told me that in parliamentary debate, audience participation plays a huge role in determining the outcome. That means when one of our debaters makes a point that really lands with you, positively or negatively, you gotta make some noise. This can be stomping your feet, smacking the armrest of your chair, whistling, cheering, hissing, booing. So, let's run a test right now. If Heidi or Rosdely says something you love, what are you gonna do?

(The audience responds.)

And if they say something you hate, what are you gonna do?

(The audience responds.)

Very nice. One more thing: At the end of this debate, one of you is gonna be selected to pick the winner, so pay attention!

(Mike gives the debaters an update on time left, then steps to the side while the debaters continue to prepare.)

Thirty seconds. *(Still timing)* Fifteen seconds.

(After the time is up, Mike rings the bell.)

Are you ready?

<table>
<tr><td align="center">ROSDELY</td><td align="center">HEIDI</td></tr>
<tr><td>Yes.</td><td>Yep.</td></tr>
</table>

MIKE

(To the audience) I'll remind the audience to please partici-pate with passion. You are not just spectators here. You can really influence the outcome of this thing. Let's do one more test. If one of our debaters says something that you both hate and love, what are you gonna do?

(The audience responds.)

Will the Proposition please approach?

(Heidi stands facing Mike, who now sits with the audience.)

[Note: The following debate points were prepared ahead of time, but the debate changes on any given night, so the debate points may not entirely reflect what actually happens on stage in the moment. This script also contains an additional debate transcript in which Heidi argues to keep the Constitution and the champion high-school debater argues to abolish.]

You have two minutes. Your time begins now.

(Heidi launches in, speaking as quickly, yet as clearly, as possible:)

HEIDI

Good evening, Judges. My name is Heidi Schreck and I'm here to represent the proposition: "This House Ought to Abolish the Constitution of the United States."

Would you please raise your hand if you are a white man who also owns property? Under the original terms of this document, you are the only people in this room who are considered citizens. How would the rest of you feel if they went into another room and made all the rules for the rest of us? Here, let's flip through the Constitution to reveal the exact page on which the rest of us become full human beings in the eyes of this document. I'm right here on page thirty-four—

ROSDELY

Point of order! You can't use props in a debate.

MIKE

Noted.

HEIDI

Fine. Thirty-four. My second point, Judges, is this: The dead should not govern the living. Thomas Jefferson himself said we should draft a new Constitution for every generation; we should not be living by the laws of corpses. The framers have been in their graves for over two hundred years. They lived in a world without indoor plumbing, electricity. They took like two baths a year. George Washington died because he had a cold and decided to treat it with bloodletting! So why are we listening to him? We should be looking at the world with our own eyes, deciding what we believe to be right and wrong, not going back ten generations to try to figure out what Alexander Hamilton would have done. It's as if we are being ruled by zombies. End zombie law. Thank you, Judges.

(Mike rings the bell. Rosdely steps into position.)

ROSDELY

Hello, Judges. My name is Rosdely Ciprian and I am the first opposition speaker to the motion that we should abolish the United States Constitution. I will first refute my opponent's points and then, if time allows, present points of my own.

My opponent quotes Thomas Jefferson, who said that the dead should not govern the living. But Thomas Jefferson himself is dead so WHY IS SHE LISTENING TO HIM?

The Proposition also says she wants to make an all-new Constitution. But who gets to make this new perfect utopian Constitution? Will kids be involved? Do you want me to go into another room and decide what's best for all of you? No you don't! This new Constitution will be made by politicians, and since Congress is still made up of mostly old white men, what are the chances they will write a better Constitution? I'll tell you what they are: about 10 scrillion to 1—the same chance that the actual zombies from *The Walking Dead* will take over our planet.

Now for my first argument: "The Constitution Is the Key to Our Liberation."

We have the oldest active Constitution in the world. My opponent wants you to think this is a bad thing, but the reason it has lasted so long is because it gives us, "We the People," the tools we need to free ourselves from tyranny, and we need these tools right now. It is undeniable that America is more equal and democratic than it was two hundred and thirty years ago. In fact, a hundred and fifty years ago it would've been illegal for you and I, as women, to be having this debate in public. It is because of the Constitution, and not in spite of it, that she and I can stand up here today and imagine a better future for our country.

The great abolitionist Frederick Douglass had more reason to hate this document than most Americans. And yet he supported it because it, quote, "contained the means to mount a critique of slavery from within." End quote.

Judges, a zombie is someone who has no connection to their past. They think about one thing: eating brains. If we throw away our own history, we are the ones who will become the Walking Dead. Thank you.

(Mike rings the bell.)

MIKE

Abolish will have one minute for rebuttal.

HEIDI

Judges, my opponent's point that Jefferson is dead, so why should we listen to him? —I uh. I'm gonna give her that. I will also grant that I do not yet have a plan about who will create this new document, but I would like to say for the record, I would love for brilliant young women like Rosdely to be involved.

69

Pandering!

HEIDI

My opponent argues that our country is more equal and democratic than it was two hundred and thirty years ago. However, we are no longer considered a full democracy. That's right. In 2017, we were demoted by the International Democracy Index. We fall below countries like Spain, Uruguay, and Mauritius.

This is because voter suppression is rampant and was basically just endorsed by our Supreme Court; two of our presidents in the past twenty years did not win the popular vote, the electoral college is an impediment to democracy, nine unelected people have decision-making power over our basic human rights, and because every day in this country, this Constitution fails to protect communities of color, LGBTQIA folx, people with disabilities, immigrants, indigenous peoples, and women!

(Mike rings the bell.)

Thank you.

MIKE

Keep, you will have thirty seconds to cross-examine.

ROSDELY

Where do you think we would land on the Democracy Index if we abolished our Constitution tomorrow?

HEIDI

Look, I don't know about tomorrow but—

ROSDELY

Don't you think we'll be *lower* than we are now?

HEIDI

If we don't make fundamental changes—

ROSDELY

But you do believe *now* is the right time to abolish our Constitution. Like, *right now?*

HEIDI

I never said we should do it right now!

ROSDELY

When should we do it then? Don't you think this *(Holds up Constitution)* is what holds us together as Americans?

HEIDI

Props! She's using props!

(Mike rings the bell and continues to ring it if either debater goes over time.)

MIKE

Time. Time! Keep will have one minute for rebuttal.

ROSDELY

Judges, I agree that we have moved backward on some issues. But we all know there are ebbs and flows to progress. I would like to remind you all of the woman and dog running along the beach. Yes, I was listening from backstage.

This brings me to my final argument: If we abolish the Constitution, we risk sending the country into *complete chaos*. Our country is more divided than it has ever been. The only thing holding us together right now as Americans is faith in this document. We may choose to interpret it differently, but without it we risk complete collapse. If we abolish the Constitution tomorrow, here is what will happen. Same-sex marriage would be illegal in fourteen states. Abortion would be illegal in thirty states. Segregation would technically be legal in thirty-two states.

Judges, this document is the only thing protecting most of us right now. Abraham Lincoln said the people should not throw out the Constitution, but to throw out the men who abuse it.

(Mike rings the bell.)

MIKE

Abolish, you have thirty seconds to cross-examine.

HEIDI

Many European countries have made brand-new constitutions peacefully. Why are you so sure we can't do the same?

ROSDELY

Because our country is more diverse than those countries. We might not have the same peaceful outcome, and that's a risk I'm not willing to take.

HEIDI

Yes, but don't you agree that the Supreme Court could roll back most of the rights you just listed even if we keep this Constitution?

ROSDELY

NO, I don't agree. Because Supreme Court decisions establish something called precedents, and those precedents are very strong.

HEIDI

The Supreme Court just overturned precedent a few months ago.

ROSDELY

I believe that was an exception—

HEIDI

I think that you're wrong—

(Mike rings the bell.)

ROSDELY

Well, I think that you're wrong! Thank you.

MIKE

Time. Each side will have one minute to conclude. Starting with Abolish.

HEIDI

Judges. As a kid, I believed this document was a tool of justice. I knew it was created by slaveholders. By people who did not consider most of us as fully human. But I believed in its genius and in its ability to transform over time. Today, however—I actually don't think our Constitution is failing. I think it is doing exactly what it was designed to do from the beginning, which is to protect the interests of a small number of rich, white men.

I believe we need a brand-new positive-rights Constitution that is designed to actively rectify the inequality at the heart of this country and to actively protect human rights, and finally our planet. Because if we don't do that, there is no future for any of us. I also believe that to have a negative-rights Constitution—a "neutral" Constitution—is to have a Constitution that continues to perpetuate the status quo in this country, and therefore perpetuates white supremacy and misogyny and violence.

Judges, why should most of us be banished to the margins of this document? Why should we remain on page thirty? On page thirty-four? Or nowhere in the document at all *(Gesturing to Rosdely)* because we're kids. We all belong in the preamble. Thank you.

ROSDELY

Judges, my opponent wants to endanger people's lives for the sake of some utopian document that hasn't even been written yet. She has the luxury for this thought experiment, most other people do not. It's going to be my generation, my community, that will have to be the guinea pigs for this grand experiment. It is my future she wants to put at risk, and I'm not going to stand for that.

Throwing out the Constitution doesn't mean we would be throwing out sexism or racism. It would be, at best, a superficial change. Democracy is not something that happens to us because we magically change a piece of paper. Democracy is something *we* have to make happen, *we* have to fight for, every single day. If you want to change the country, you need to wake up. Run for local office, run for student government. Protest. Put pressure on your representatives.

Start with your own personal Constitution and build your way out. Thank you.

(Heidi joins Rosdely center stage and they shake hands.)

HEIDI

Now it's time to choose our judge. Rosdely will be choosing our judge.

(Rosdely chooses an audience member from the front row to be the judge. Ideally, the front-row tickets are sold at a discount to young people. If an audience member declines the honor, Rosdely or Heidi may say: "This is how democracy dies.")

ROSDELY

Hi. Would you mind being our judge?

AUDIENCE MEMBER

Uh, sure.

ROSDELY

What's your name? Where are you from?

AUDIENCE MEMBER

Amber. I'm from southwest Missouri.

ROSDELY

Whoa. Wow.

HEIDI

Do you mind standing up for us, Amber?

(Heidi turns to the audience:)

Since we don't live in a real democracy, Amber will be representing all of your interests. *(To Amber)* Okay, Amber, you have such an important decision to make: to keep or abolish the United States Constitution.

(Heidi hands Amber two envelopes. One is labeled "Keep" and the other "Abolish.")

We would love for you to make your decision in silence and then open the corresponding envelope and read the official language out loud to "the people." That way it's legal. We'll be over here so we can't see what you're deciding.

(Rosdely and Heidi move to the side as Amber opens one of the envelopes.)

AMBER

On behalf of the audience of *What the Constitution Means to Me*, I, Amber, do hereby vote to keep the Constitution.

(Some audience members cheer, some boo. Heidi turns to the audience:)

HEIDI

Okay, fine. Since you voted to keep it, you can keep your pocket Constitutions, too. Take those home with you. We're now at the end of our evening, but we always do one final thing after we debate.

ROSDELY

Heidi and I ask each other a couple of questions to get to know one another as human beings. These questions were submitted to us by last night's audience. Feel free to write your own questions on the way out.

(Mike trots down and hands Heidi the question cards. Rosdely turns to the stage manager's booth:)

Terri?

TERRI
(From the booth) Yeah?

ROSDELY
Can you please dim the lights?

TERRI
(From the booth) Absolutely. Here you go.

[Note: Each night, Heidi and the young debater receive a curated set of questions that audience members have submitted. They answer the questions extemporaneously. The young debater always answers the final question, which is planted. It should always be some kind of question about how the young debater imagines her future—in ten years, in fifty years, etc. The following is a transcript from the Clubbed Thumb production in June 2017 at the Wild Project in New York City.]

(Rosdely and Heidi sit back-to-back in the semi-darkness.)

ROSDELY
(Reading from the card) If you had to win a dance contest, what song would you pick to dance to and why?

HEIDI

Uh . . . Well as you know from the other night, I really always wanted to be a prima ballerina. So, um . . . I would dance to "The Dying . . ." I would dance "The Dying Swan."

ROSDELY

(Skeptical) Oh . . . okay.

HEIDI

(Reading from the card) Rosdely, what is your favorite holiday and why?

ROSDELY

Oh, this is easy. My favorite holiday is Christmas. I get to watch movies nonstop, I get to drink hot chocolate. We sing songs and I get presents and I get to spend some time with family and sometimes we do a nice family dinner.

HEIDI

(Reading from the card) What do you have at your family dinner?

ROSDELY

Oh, a lot of good stuff. Some lasagna, some roast pork, some rice, egg or potato salad . . . I don't . . . I can never tell the difference between egg salad and potato salad.

(Reading from the card) Heidi, what was one of your fattest teachers . . . wait . . . *favorite* teachers and why?

HEIDI

Um . . . My favorite teacher was Ms. Perkins. She was my tenth grade P.E. teacher. She wore . . . she drove a Corvette with a personalized license plate that read "MsPerkins." And she was gay, but she couldn't be out in our town at that time, and we all adored her.

ROSDELY

Okay.

HEIDI

(Reading from the card) Rosdely, what's your favorite movie?

ROSDELY

Oooh. My fa . . . I can't choose. Either *White Chicks* . . . yeah, *White Chicks*.

(Reading from the card) Heidi, if time and money were no obstacle, what's one thing you would want to do?

HEIDI

Uh . . . Wow. Huh. If time and money were no . . . *(Beat)* If time isn't an obstacle, I want to time travel.

(Reading from the card) Rosdely, what do you imagine your life will be like in thirty years?

ROSDELY

Oh, I uh— In thirty years . . . I'll be? Forty-four. Whoa. I'll be . . . yeah. Old. Hopefully, I'll be done with college. Maybe I'll be an actress. Or a pediatrician. And I'll have a nice house. And I'll have a kid. One kid. I don't want . . . I definitely don't want more than one because, ugh, kids. Stressful. And I'll . . . I'll be pretty happy. Yeah. Uh. That's what I imagine.

(Beat. Terri dims the lights.)

ALTERNATE DEBATE

The following is a transcript of a performance starring debater Thursday Williams, who alternated performances with Rosdely Ciprian on Broadway. On this night, Thursday argued to abolish the United States Constitution and Heidi argued to keep it.

THURSDAY
Hi. My name is Thursday Williams. I am a senior at William Cullen Bryant High School and I am a member of the Legal Outreach Program where I practice constitutional debate. I am also a proud member of the Explorers Program with the 103rd Precinct. I spent this past summer working in the Queens Supreme Court as part of the Sonia and Celina Sotomayor Judicial Internship Program. Heidi invited me here tonight to debate a big question about the Constitution: Is it protecting us, or is it the source of our problems? Person-

ally, I think the answer is *both*, but for the sake of having a good debate, we are each going to take a different side here tonight.

Before I explain to you the rules of our debate, let me say that the Constitution is not a crucible. At least that's not how I like to think of it. Why not just think of the Constitution as a human being? It was created by human beings so it's not a big stretch. Are human beings perfect? No. Are we capable of perfection? No. Just like us, this document is flawed. But just like us, it is also capable of getting better. And better. With every generation.

Now it's possible that I may have to argue against this. And that's fine. I'm happy to do that. But I want to be honest about what I really think first.

My opponent brought up the 9th Amendment in her pre-pared speech which went way over time by the way. The penumbra metaphor is an interesting way to understand the 9th Amendment. I am not arguing against it, but let me help you understand it another way.

When I visited court for the first time this summer, this top-notch lawyer walked into the courtroom wearing red-soled shoes. She automatically took control of the room. It's as if she was saying: "You all better listen to me because I know what I'm talking about." She was confident about every word that came out her mouth. To be honest, she made the rest of the lawyers look like amateurs. And as I watched her, I thought: "I want those shoes."

(Thursday shows the audience her fancy shoes.)

I am just gonna go ahead and say those shoes are my 9th Amendment. They're gonna take me into the future. But of course, I won't know what that looks like till I get there.

Okay, let's start this debate!

HEIDI

Let's do it! For the past year, Thursday and I have been doing parliamentary-style debate together, which is a style that did not exist when I was in high school. And we're going to do a real, live debate for you—right here right now.

THURSDAY

The topic of this debate is: "Should We Abolish the United States Constitution?"

(The ushers pass out pocket Constitutions to the audience during the following exchange. There should be one pocket Constitution for each audience member.)

HEIDI

There are people passing out pocket Constitutions for you to use, so you can follow along, check our work.

THURSDAY

Usually in debate there are three people on a team, but tonight we are going to do this one-on-one. This is a version we like to call "Iron Man." Usually, in parliamentary debate we do a form called PO-POOP which is "Proposition, opposition-proposition, opposition, opposition, proposition," but we've created our own style that we are calling POPOPO: "Proposition, opposition, proposition, opposition, proposition, opposition."

MIKE

The debaters have been training me to be the moderator and my most important duty is to flip a coin to determine which side of the argument our debaters will take.

Thursday, please call it in the air.

(Mike flips a coin. Thursday and Heidi call out heads or tails. Mike turns to the person who wins the coin toss.)

[Note: Thursday and Heidi have developed their arguments through a year of debating extemporaneously together, and portions of this debate change from night to night. The following is a transcript from a performance at The Helen Hayes Theater in New York City in March 2019.]

Heads it is, which side would you like to take?

THURSDAY

Proposition: "Abolish."

HEIDI

Opposition: "Keep."

MIKE

Okay. Debaters, you have ninety seconds to prepare. Starting now.

(Heidi and Thursday rush to sit at two card tables that Mike has set up for them. The tables are covered with index cards, legal pads, pens, highlighters, water, and other supplies they might need. They prepare in silence, writing their points on index cards, etc.)

Thursday has also told me that in parliamentary debate, audience participation plays a huge role in determining the outcome. That means when one of these debaters makes a point that really lands with you, positively or negatively, you gotta make some noise. You can do this by stomping your feet, smacking the armrest of your chair, cheering or booing. So, let's run a test right now. If Heidi or Thursday says something you love, what are you gonna do?

(The audience responds.)

And if they say something you hate, what are you gonna do?

(The audience responds.)

Very nice. One more thing: At the end of this debate, one of you is gonna be selected to pick the winner, so please pay attention!

(Mike gives the debaters an update on time left, then steps to the side while the debaters continue to prepare.)

Thirty seconds. *(Still timing)* Fifteen seconds.

(After the time is up, Mike rings the bell.)

Are you ready?

THURSDAY		HEIDI
Yes.	Yep.	

MIKE
(To the audience) I'll remind you to please participate with passion. You are not just spectators here. You can really

influence the outcome of this thing. Let's do one more test. This time, let's hear what it sounds like if they say something that you both hate and love.

(The audience responds.)

Will the Proposition please approach?

(Heidi stands facing Mike, who now sits with the audience.)

[Note: The following debate points were prepared ahead of time, but the debate changes on any given night, so the debate points may not entirely reflect what actually happens on stage in the moment. This script also contains an additional debate transcript in which Heidi argues to abolish the Constitution and the champion high-school debater argues to keep.]

You have two minutes. Your time begins now.

THURSDAY

Good evening, Judges. My name is Thursday Williams and I represent the proposition: "This House Ought to Abolish the United States Constitution." Thank you.

Everyone, please raise your hand. Raise your hand, raise your hand. Now, if you're a white man who owns property, please put your hand down. Under the original terms of the Constitution, those of us with our hands up are not considered citizens. Let me ask you a question: How would you feel if these white men went into another room and made all the rules for the rest of us?!

That's what I thought! You can put your hands down now. Why don't you look through your pocket Constitution to see where people like us belong . . . You, ma'am, you're probably right here on page thirty-four . . .

HEIDI

Point of order! We're not supposed to use props in a debate!

MIKE

Noted.

THURSDAY

"Point of order!"? The real point of order is my opponent advocating for a document that doesn't even protect her. But fine—thirty-four.

Moving on. My second point: The dead should not govern the living. Thomas Jefferson himself said that we should draft a new Constitution for every generation. The framers have been in their graves for over two hundred years. They lived in a world without toothbrushes, deodorant, and toilet paper. The great Benjamin Franklin didn't even take a bath with fresh water, but instead took something called an "air bath," where he would walk around naked, thinking that the air would bathe him. Our very own George Washington died because he had a cold and decided to treat it with bloodletting. So please tell me, why are we listening to "Air Bath" Franklin and "Bloodletting" Washington?

We should be looking at the world with our own eyes, deciding what you and I believe to be right and wrong. Not going back ten generations to figure out what Alexander Hamilton would've done. Thank you.

HEIDI

Hello, Judges. My name is Heidi Schreck. I am the first opposition speaker to the motion that we should abolish the United States Constitution. My opponent, who is young, quotes Thomas Jefferson, who said that the dead should not govern the living, but Thomas Jefferson himself is dead. So why is she listening to him?

She also says that she's going to make an all new Constitution for every generation. But who gets to make this brand-new, perfect utopian Constitution? Will those of us who had our hands up get to make it? I don't think so! This new Constitution will be made by politicians, and since Congress is still made up of mostly old white men, why does she think they will write a better Constitution?

Now for my first argument: "The Constitution Is the Key to Our Liberation."

Judges, we have the oldest living Constitution in the world. My opponent wants you to think that is a bad thing, but the reason it has lasted so long is because it gives "We the People" the tools we need to free ourselves from tyranny. And we need those tools right now. It is undeniable that America is more equal and more democratic than it was two hundred and thirty years ago. In fact, you know what? One hundred and fifty years ago, it would've been illegal for my opponent and I, as women, to be having this debate in public. It is because of the Constitution, not in spite of it, that we can stand up here today and insist on a better future for our country. Thank you.

MIKE

Abolish, you have one minute for rebuttal.

THURSDAY

Judges, my opponent's point that Thomas Jefferson is dead so why should we listen to him? I'm gonna give her that one. I will also grant that I do not yet have a plan for who will create this new document, but I do know that it will not be fully created by white men. Apparently, my opponent (who is much older) isn't aware of the recent changes in our government. Congress is more diverse than it has ever been and I have faith that people like me will be involved in this redesigning process—whether these men like it or not.

My opponent argued that we are more equal and democratic than we were two hundred and thirty years ago. That dog on the beach metaphor is simply an illusion. Look at the 13th Amendment, for example: It abolished slavery only for it to be reimagined as a prison industry that is a new systemic form of oppression. A felon is not equal to me. Even after serving their time, even after being "rehabilitated," a felon cannot vote. A felon cannot serve on a jury. Does that sound like we're moving forward to you? Well, there's more. Today, the electoral college is a hot mess! Two of our last three presidents did not win the popular vote! Different branches of our government are overstepping their powers. Voter suppression is rampant. Nine people have disproportionate power over our basic human rights. And communities of color, women, LGBTQIA folx, people with disabilities, and immigrants have their human rights violated on a daily basis. Thank you.

MIKE

Keep, you have thirty seconds to cross-examine.

HEIDI

You say that progress is an illusion, but here we are debating. Don't you agree that this is progress?

THURSDAY

That's just one example of progress. There are many other issues where we've actually gone backwards. I mean, it's funny because I actually have fewer rights than you had when you were my age. Since I was born, there have been over two hundred laws that have rolled back women's reproductive rights. That is not progress!

HEIDI

Yes but our Constitution was designed to evolve and change. So why don't we protect those rights by passing an amendment—

THURSDAY

Amendments take too long! We've been trying to pass an Equal Rights Amendment for over one hundred years!

HEIDI

We're one state away. I'm not ready to give up yet—

THURSDAY

How many amendments have been passed in your lifetime?

HEIDI

Uh. One, I think. The 27th Amendment.

Yeah and that took two hundred and thirty years to pass. I don't think you've got another hundred and thirty years in you, Heidi.

(Mike rings the bell.)

I rest my case.

MIKE

Keep, you have one minute for rebuttal.

HEIDI

Judges. I agree that we have moved backwards on some issues, but my opponent is confusing illusion with the natural ebbs and flows of progress. If we throw out this document, we throw out the actual progress that the generations before us fought so hard to achieve. If we abolish the Constitution tomorrow, here's what would happen: Same-sex marriage would be illegal in fourteen states. Abortion would be illegal in thirty states. Segregation would technically be legal in thirty-two states. The only thing holding us together right now as a country is a collective faith in this document. Yes, we might interpret it differently, but without it we risk complete collapse.

Judges, Abraham Lincoln said we should not overthrow the Constitution, but to overthrow the men who abuse it. Thank you.

MIKE

Abolish, you have thirty seconds to cross-examine.

THURSDAY

Would you agree that the Supreme Court could roll back all the rights you just listed even if we keep the Constitution?

HEIDI

I do agree. That's why we need to do the hard work of passing amendments. To protect our basic human rights from the whims of a partisan court.

THURSDAY

Again, we don't have time! How long do you think it's gonna take to get a climate change amendment?

HEIDI

You keep talking about time. I don't know, but the fact is that I don't believe it's gonna take longer to amend it than it would to write a whole new Constitution.

THURSDAY

We're gonna be extinct!

(Mike rings the bell.)

MIKE

Time! Each side will have one minute to conclude. Starting with Abolish.

THURSDAY

Judges, as a young immigrant woman of color, I used to believe in this document. I believed it had the power to protect me. It gave me the right to vote, the right to no longer be considered property. But as I've gotten older, I have come to realize that this document does not protect me. It never did and it never will.

Civil Rights activist Dorothy Height said: "I believe we hold in our hands the power to once again shape not only our own, but the nation's future." We need a new positive-rights document that is easy to understand and that actually includes people like you and me from the very beginning. I want a document that says health care is a human right, that protects education as a fundamental pillar for our society, that truly considers all human beings as equal and that actively protects our planet. Because without that, there is no future for any of us.

I am one of this generation's founding daughters and I'm telling you we need a change. Thank you.

HEIDI

Judges, the truth is that I totally agree with my opponent. In a perfect world, I would love to scrap this document and make a brand-new positive-rights document that actively includes all of us. However, I sadly don't think there's a way to do this without endangering all of our rights.

Judges, democracy is not something that just happens to us because we magically change a piece of paper. Democracy is something that we have to fight for, that we have to make happen, that we have to keep alive every day.

The great Civil Rights activist Diane Nash said: "Freedom is, by definition, people realizing that they are their own leaders." Let us petition our lawmakers to write and pass a climate change amendment, let's pass the Equal Rights Amendment. Or you know what? Better yet, let's run for Congress ourselves! Thursday Williams, I am ready to start knocking on doors for you!

THURSDAY

Pandering!

HEIDI

Fine, I'm pandering. But it's also true. Thank you!

(They shake hands.)

THURSDAY

It's time for us to choose a judge and I will be making that decision tonight. *(She scans the audience and chooses a woman from the front row)* Hi! Would you like to be our judge for tonight?

JUDGE

Uh. Sure.

THURSDAY

What is your name?

JUDGE

Nicole.

THURSDAY

Hi, Nicole. Where are you from?

NICOLE

Astoria.

THURSDAY

Oh! I go to school in Astoria! Bryant High School.

HEIDI

Do you mind standing up for us?

NICOLE

Okay.

HEIDI

Thank you so much. *(To the audience)* All right, since we don't live in an actual democracy, Nicole will be representing all of your interests. Okay, Nicole, you have a very important decision to make: to abolish or keep the Constitution. We would love for you to make your decision in silence and then open the corresponding envelope and read the official language out loud, to the people. That way the spell is real and it's legal. We'll be over here, so we can't see what you're deciding.

(Heidi hands Nicole two envelopes. One is labeled "Keep" and the other "Abolish.")

NICOLE

Um. Okay I think I know what I wanna— You were both great by the way. It's a tough choice.

HEIDI

It's not legally binding.

NICOLE

Okay, well um. On this night, March 23rd, 2019, I, Nicole, on behalf of the audience of *What the Constitution Means to Me*, do hereby vote to abolish the Constitution.

(Some audience members cheer, some boo. Heidi turns to the audience:)

HEIDI

Thank you, all right. Wonderful! Since Nicole voted to abolish, you can go ahead and take your pocket Constitutions home so that you have something to read when you're in your bunker.

THURSDAY

We are now at the end of our evening, but we like to do one final thing after we debate. Heidi and I just ask each other a few questions to get to know one another better as human beings. These questions were left by last night's audience. Feel free to leave your own questions for us on the way out.

(Mike hands Thursday and Heidi the questions from last night's audience. Thursday turns to talk to the stage manager.)

Arabella?

ARABELLA

(From the booth) Yes?

THURSDAY

Can you please dim the lights?

ARABELLA

Oh, absolutely. Here we go!

THURSDAY

Thank you.

HEIDI

Not too dim!

[Note: Each night, Heidi and the young debater receive a curated set of questions that audience members have submitted. They answer the questions extemporaneously. The young debater always answers the final question, which is planted. It should always be some kind of question about how the young debater imagines her future—in ten years, in fifty years, etc.]

(They sit on the edge of the stage, back to back, in the shadows.)

THURSDAY

Do you want me to go first?

HEIDI

Sure.

THURSDAY

(Reading from the card) Are you superstitious about anything?

HEIDI

Yeah, so many things! I don't know if you've seen me do it, but if I drop the script on the floor or any part of the debate cards, I have to turn around three times and air spit. Because there's this Russian superstition that if you drop a page of the script, that you'll never be able to peform that page well.

(Reading from the card) Thursday, if you were ever going to get a tattoo, what would it be?

THURSDAY

(Laughs) Can I pass?

HEIDI

Absolutely!

THURSDAY

Actually, I think . . . you remember before I come out on stage, that RBG quote? I think I'd get that quote right here on this arm.

(She reads the next question) What is the best trait to have in a friend?

HEIDI

Uh, the best trait in a friend—I'm gonna say first loyalty, followed by a sense of humor.

(She reads the next question) Um, Thursday, what is the most expensive thing you've ever broken?

THURSDAY

I don't . . . oh, I know! So, my grandmother has a—a—a— it's a . . . I don't know how to describe it. It's like—she puts all of her drinking glasses, 'cause she buys, I don't understand her point of buying glasses just to put them up for decoration—but she has a whole part for that and it's just drinking glasses. And I was playing ball in the house one day . . . and we all know how that story ends.

(She reads the next question) How do you think entertainment will change in the next hundred years?

HEIDI

I don't know, but I imagine that maybe we could just like, just give each other movies with our thoughts. Like I could be like "here's a movie" and then you and I just think it to each other, maybe?

(She reads the final question) Okay Thursday, this is your last question. Oh wow, okay. What do you imagine your life will be like in ten years?

THURSDAY

Oh, that's close. Um, so ten years . . . I will be twenty-seven, about to be twenty-eight in like a month. Okay, so I've already graduated undergrad and law school. So I'll be in the House, 'cause that's what I plan to do immediately after grad school. And I might stay there for a couple of years, because we all know we need to stay there for a couple years. And also at twenty-eight, I think I'll be starting to develop my Woman's Empowerment Program that I've been dreaming of since freshman year of high school. And so, I think that will be launching hopefully when I'm twenty-eight. On a personal note, I don't think I want any spouse, not at twenty-eight. I would like a dog. And I think, unfortunately, I'll still be living in New York City and depending on the MTA. And maybe I'll be thinking about going back to school for my PhD. I don't know . . . Yeah. That's what I imagine.

(Beat. Arabella dims the lights.)

END

SUGGESTED READING

The following is a reading list of research materials that were used in the creation of this play.

BOOKS

About Abortion: Terminating Pregnancy in Twenty-First-Century America, by Carol Sanger (The Belknap Press of Harvard University Press, 2017).

African Americans and the Living Constitution, edited by John Hope Franklin and Genna Rae McNeil (Smithsonian, 1995).

All the Single Ladies: Unmarried Women and the Rise of an Independent Nation, by Rebecca Traister (Simon & Schuster, 2016).

Black Resistance/White Law: A History of Constitutional Racism in America, by Mary Frances Berry (Penguin, 1971, 1994).

The Conduct of Life, by Maria Irene Fornes (*Plays: Maria Irene Fornes*, PAJ Publications, 2001).

The Constitution of the Czech Republic (1992).

The Constitution of the Republic of South Africa (1996).

Equal Means Equal: Why the Time for an Equal Rights Amendment Is Now, by Jessica Neuwirth (The New Press, 2015).

Fault Lines in the Constitution: The Framers, Their Fights, and the Flaws That Affect Us Today, by Cynthia Levinson and Sanford Levinson (Peachtree Publishing Company, 2017).

The Invisible Constitution, by Laurence H. Tribe (Oxford University Press, 2008).

Men Explain Things to Me, by Rebecca Solnit (Haymarket Books, 2014).

My Own Words, by Ruth Bader Ginsburg with Mary Hartnett and Wendy W. Williams (Simon & Schuster, 2016).

Notorious RBG: The Life and Times of Ruth Bader Ginsburg, by Irin Carmon and Shana Knizhnik (HarperCollins Publishers, 2015).

The Race of the Ark Tattoo, by W. David Hancock (a play, unpublished, 1998).

Retained by the People: The "Silent" Ninth Amendment and the Constitutional Rights Americans Don't Know They Have, by Daniel A. Farber (Basic Books, 2007).

Song in a Weary Throat: Memoir of an American Pilgrimage, by Pauli Murray (Liveright Publishing Corporation of W. W. Norton & Company, 1987, 2018).

Trauma and Recovery: The Aftermath of Violence—From Domestic Abuse to Political Terror, by Judith Herman, M.D. (Basic Books, 1992, 2015).

2.5 Minute Ride, by Lisa Kron (Theatre Communications Group, 2000).

The Universal Declaration of Human Rights (United Nations, 1948).

The Warren Court and American Politics, by Lucas A. Powe, Jr. (The Belknap Press of Harvard University Press, 2002).

Wild Bill: The Legend and Life of William O. Douglas (America's Most Controversial Supreme Court Justice), by Bruce Allen Murphy (Random House, 2003).

Women in Pacific Northwest History, edited by Karen J. Blair (University of Washington Press, 2001).

ARTICLES

"The Death of the Fourteenth Amendment: Castle Rock and Its Progeny," by G. Kristian Miccio (*William & Mary Jour-*

nal of Race, Gender, and Social Justice; Volume 17 [2010–2011], Issue 2, Article 2, *William & Mary Journal of Women and the Law*; February 2011).

"To Have and Hold: Reproduction, Marriage, and the Constitution," by Jill Lepore (*New Yorker*, May 18, 2015 and May 25, 2015 Dept. of Justice Issue).

"U.S. in Top 10 Most Dangerous Countries for Women, Report Finds," by David Brennan (*Newsweek*, June 26, 2018).

SPEECHES

"The Bicentennial Speech," by Justice Thurgood Marshall (delivered in Maui, Hawaii, on May 6, 1987, as part of the constitutional bicentennial celebration at The Annual Seminar of the San Francisco Patent and Trademark Law Association).

OTHER

Much of the research for this play was done with the help of oyez.org, a free law project supported through Cornell's Legal Information Institute, justia.com, and Chicago-Kent College of Law. Oyez is a terrific website that makes recordings of Supreme Court cases accessible to the public for free.

HEIDI SCHRECK is a writer and performer living in Brooklyn. *What the Constitution Means to Me* was named a Pulitzer Prize finalist, won the Obie Award and New York Drama Critics' Circle Award for Best American Play, and was nominated for a Tony Award for Best Play. Schreck also received a Tony Award nomination for Best Performance by an Actress in a Leading Role in a Play. After an extended run on Broadway, *What the Constitution Means to Me* played a sold-out, limited run at the Kennedy Center in Washington, DC, and at the Mark Taper Forum in Los Angeles. Its national tour will resume in 2021.

What the Constitution Means to Me was named Best of the Year by *New York Times*, *Los Angeles Times*, *Chicago Tribune*, *TIME*, *Hollywood Reporter*, *New Yorker*, *Newsweek*, *BuzzFeed*, *Forbes*, *Washington Post*, and *Entertainment Weekly*. NPR named it one of the "50 Great Pop Culture Moments" of 2019.

Schreck's other plays include: *Grand Concourse*, *Creature*, and *There Are No More Big Secrets*. Her screenwriting credits include *I Love Dick*, *Billions*, and *Nurse Jackie*. She has shows in development with Amazon, Big Beach, Imagine Television, and A24.

She is the recipient of three Obie Awards, a Drama Desk Award, a Theatre World Award, a Horton Foote Playwriting Award, and the Hull-Warriner Award. She was named one of *Fast Company*'s "Most Creative People in Business" in 2019, and was featured on *Variety*'s 2019 Broadway Impact List. Schreck was awarded *Smithsonian* magazine's 2019 American Ingenuity Award. She received the 2019 Benjamin Hadley Danks Award from the Academy of Arts and Letters.

Theatre Communications Group would like to offer our special thanks to Heather Randall and the Tony Randall Theatrical Fund for their generous support of the publication of
What the Constitution Means to Me *by Heidi Schreck*

HEATHER RANDALL serves as Chairwoman and Executive Director of the Tony Randall Theatrical Fund, dedicated to supporting not-for-profit theatre companies and service organizations, innovative productions, and initiatives in arts education and arts-based community-outreach programs. Heather is a former TCG board member and a member of the National Council for the American Theatre.

Heather believes in fighting for the rights, safety, and dignity of women. She understands this play's timely resonance with this fight, and proudly supports widening access to Heidi Schreck's deeply personal and political exploration.

TCG books sponsored by Heather and the Tony Randall Theatrical Fund include:

Jeremy O. Harris, *Slave Play*
Heidi Schreck, *What the Constitution Means to Me*

THEATRE COMMUNICATIONS GROUP's mission is to lead for a just and thriving theatre ecology. Through its Core Values of Activism, Artistry, Diversity, and Global Citizenship, TCG advances a better world for theatre and a better world because of theatre. TCG Books is the largest independent trade publisher of dramatic literature in North America, with 18 Pulitzer Prizes for Best Play on its book list. The book program commits to the life-long career of its playwrights, keeping all of their plays in print. TCG Books' other authors include: Annie Baker, Nilo Cruz, Jackie Sibblies Drury, Athol Fugard, Quiara Alegría Hudes, David Henry Hwang, Branden Jacobs-Jenkins, Tony Kushner, Young Jean Lee, Lynn Nottage, Suzan-Lori Parks, Sarah Ruhl, Stephen Sondheim, Paula Vogel, Anne Washburn, and August Wilson, among many others.

Support TCG's work in the theatre field by becoming a member or donor: www.tcg.org

tcg